D1631411

The Challenge of Evangelical Theology

The Challenge of Evangelical Theology

Essays in Approach and Method

edited by

Nigel M. de S. Cameron
Warden of Rutherford House, Edinburgh

Rutherford House Books
Edinburgh

Published by Rutherford House,
Claremont Park, Edinburgh EH6 7PJ, Scotland

ISBN 0 946068 26 7

Copyright © 1987 Rutherford House and Contributors
This edition published 1987

All rights reserved. No part of this publication may be reproduced, stored in a retrieval system, or transmitted, in any form, by any means, electronic, mechanical, photocopying, recording or otherwise without the prior permission of Rutherford House.

Computer typeset at Rutherford House on Apple Macintosh.
Printed by Chong Moh, Singapore.

CONTENTS

PREFACE

The title of this collection of essays has been deliberately chosen. In Britain, at least, while the post-War years have seen a renaissance of conservative participation in Biblical studies, in what may reasonably be termed theology proper – historical, systematic, dogmatic, philosophical – much less has been done. Conservative evangelical *theology* has remained heavily dependent upon the considerable output, both of men and of ideas, of the churches of North America.

One of the tasks which Rutherford House has set itself is to seek to begin to redress this imbalance, and to encourage indigenous engagement in these fundamental questions, convinced that the church at large will look increasingly to conservatives for the theological leadership which the bankruptcy of alternatives to orthodoxy has let go by default.   In initiating a series of biennial conferences for conservative theologians, the *Edinburgh Conference in Christian Dogmatics*, Rutherford House has sought to respond to this need, confident that we are now possessed of intellectual resources to begin to meet the challenge of a dynamic and fresh, yet faithfully Biblical, evangelical theology.   It was to enable work of this kind to be readily disseminated that the publication was undertaken by the House, together with the Scottish Evangelical Theology Society, of the *Scottish Bulletin of Evangelical Theology*.   This volume of essays is published as a *Special Study* of the *SBET*, the first, perhaps, of a series.

Of the essays collected in this volume, all but one were originally delivered as papers to the first *Edinburgh Conference in Christian Dogmatics*, held in the summer of 1985.   Two of the writers of the essays which follow, Professor Blocher and Professor Veenhof, attended the conference as the guests of Rutherford House, since it was considered of special importance to have a European input to this first gathering; and, if they may be singled out, particular thanks are due to them for their contributions. Professor Reymond was in Britain on a period of sabbatical leave, part of which he spent as a Visiting Scholar at Rutherford House. The opening essay, by the present writer, was given as the 1986 Convocation Address at Reformed Theological Seminary, Jackson, Mississippi, and he would like to express his gratitude to RTS for their kind invitation and hospitality, and for permission to use the paper here.

Nigel M. de S. Cameron
Rutherford House
10 December 1986

THE LOGIC OF BIBLICAL AUTHORITY

NIGEL M. de S. CAMERON

One of the problems that arises from the evangelical preoccupation with the doctrine of Holy Scripture is that it encourages the deeply mistaken belief – so congenial to those outside the evangelical fold – that it is some sort of novelty; that our doctrine of Scripture is a sectarian super-addition to the faith once delivered to the saints. We need to be reminded of some words which, if they are repeated often enough, will play their part in exploding this particular myth. They were written at the height of the so-called Fundamentalist controversy of the early part of the century by that distinguished New Testament scholar who in matters theological was almost eccentrically Liberal, Kirsopp Lake, in an aside in his fascinating little book, *The Religion of Yesterday and Tomorrow*, which forms a kind of companion piece to Machen's *Christianity and Liberalism* as a popular manifesto from the other side. Lake says this:

> It is a mistake, often made by educated men who happen to have but little knowledge of historical theology, to suppose that Fundamentalism is a new and strange form of thought. It is nothing of the kind: it is the partial and uneducated survival of a theology which was once universally held by all Christians. How many were there, for instance, in the Christian churches, in the eighteenth century, who doubted the infallible inspiration of all Scripture? A few, perhaps, but very few. No, the Fundamentalist may be wrong;. I think he is. But it is we who have departed from the tradition, not he, and I am sorry for the fate of anyone who tries to argue with a Fundamentalist on the basis of authority. The Bible and the *corpus theologicum* of the church is on the Fundamentalist side.[1]

---

1. Kirsopp Lake, *The Religion of Yesterday and Tomorrow*, Boston, 1926, pp. 61,2

Lake forcefully recognises the authenticity of the orthodox tradition and its corollary – the substantial *in*authenticity of the tradition which has arisen in its place as the voice of mainstream Christianity. But he recognises also something else of at least equal importance, the *logic* of orthodoxy; the inter-relation of orthodox doctrine generally and an orthodox doctrine of Holy Scripture. This, from the point of view of method, is the question to which we now turn. It may be further illuminated with Lake's assistance. Of the new theological movement of the nineteenth century which formed the intellectual context of the challenge to orthodoxy in his day – much as it does in our own – he writes as follows:

> Since the Reformation, there has been no intellectual movement in Christianity which can compare in importance with the storm which began in the first half of the nineteenth century, and is still unabated. It has produced a general unsettlement of mind with regard to all traditional doctrine, because it has broken up the authority of the Revelation on which doctrine is based. That Revelation gave a complete account of man's history and future lot, beginning in the Garden of Eden and ending in Heaven or Hell, and this account has become completely discredited at every point where it can be reached.[2]

His candour is to be admired! He can see and will admit what is hidden from so many who would prefer to cast themselves in more moderate roles, but who are in fact simply less consequent in their thinking; that the new theology has 'broken up the authority of the Revelation' and thereby dislodged the structure of Christian doctrine 'based' upon it. That is because of the function of Holy Scripture. Listen again to Lake:

> The historic faith of the church ... is a perfectly clear and consistent whole. It is to be taken or rejected. Nothing

---

2. *Ibid.*, p. 45.

> is gained by the device of cutting out, for instance, the Virgin Birth, but accepting the doctrine of the Incarnation, or doubting the judgement to come, but insisting on the Trinity. The Incarnation is a far more difficult thing to believe than the Virgin Birth.... *The basis of this faith was not thought to be discovery by human logic but revelation by the act of God, and this revelation is to be found in the Bible, which is infallible.*[3]

And, he goes on, if this is indeed the case,

> the Bible is a direct and infallible source of knowledge, co-ordinate with reason, not subject to its criticism. What the Bible states is true, because the Bible says so; therefore if the Bible says that Jesus is the Incarnate Logos the matter is settled....

> The only alternative is that the Church of tomorrow will frankly accept the 'Experimentalist' position ... in the sense that [religion] will be based on observation, not on authority, on the facts of religion, as perceived by the individual, not on biblical or ecclesiastical revelation.[4]

The principal point, for which we are indebted to the clarity of Kirsopp Lake's exposition, is that in whatever terms the contemporary debate about the integrity of Holy Scripture is couched – and at different times swords have been drawn at the mention of inerrancy, or infallibility, or verbal or plenary inspiration – the issue to which these watchwords have been intended to draw attention is as central as it could be.

Of course, this has long been argued by advocates of the so-called domino theory – that once the doctrine of Scripture has gone the rest will fall in turn – although the credibility of this

---

3. *Ibid.*, pp. 79, 80; our emphasis.
4. *Ibid.*, pp. 145,6; 158.

kind of analysis has been put in question in the common mind by the fact that doctrinal dominos have a curious capacity to resist the dynamics of theological change. The Liberals of the 1920's – and none more than Kirsopp Lake, who was a domino theorist before his time – would have been taken aback to discover the unwonted durability of Christian doctrine in the face of assault. While the theological work of our generation has cast everything into doubt, the major denominations have remained substantially and surprisingly orthodox – including those which took the Liberal path in the years of fundamental struggle towards the end of which Lake and Machen were writing. By the same token, many have found it difficult to predicate of those who have the appearance of being evangelicals just like us, an incipient abandonment of all that they hold dear on the ground that they formulate their doctrine of Holy Scripture in a seemingly slightly different fashion. Which is not to say that the theory is mistaken, but that it needs to be advanced with more sophistication than has sometimes been afforded, taking full account of the effect of credal and confessional traditions at one remove from Scripture, and, from another perspective, of the remarkable grace of God towards his church.

But our argument is at another level. It concerns not the survival of particular doctrines, but rather the very possibility of Christian doctrine, that is, of the reception and appropriation by the church of the knowledge of God. Kirsopp Lake's contention is that the foundations of Christian doctrine in the Word of God have been discredited, such that the only remaining option is a religion based not upon revelation at all, but on what he calls 'discovery', empirical observation, the general means by which human knowledge is advanced in place of any special means. The option of revelation has been foreclosed.

Is the choice of alternatives with which Kirsopp Lake presents us finally valid? Are these the only logical options in theology? Insofar as there has been any consensus in modern Protestant theology, it has had the effect of denying Lake's argument, asserting rather a middle way in which theological endeavour can result in the knowledge of God without resort either, on the one hand, to a concept of mere human discovery as the ground of religious authority or, on the other, to the orthodox doctrine of Holy Scripture.

Henry Longueville Mansel was an Oxford philosopher of the middle nineteenth century. Though not an evangelical, he emerged as a potent defender of the heartland of Christian orthodoxy in those years of ferment to which Kirsopp Lake was later to refer. It was, alas, the case, that while the mid-Victorian years were something of an evangelical hey-day in Britain, the Tractarian controversy in England absorbed many of the best evangelical energies, and left other – and ultimately more significant – questions to go largely by default. Certainly the best defences of orthodoxy which mid-Victorian England produced were not the work of evangelicals. So it was with Henry Longueville Mansel.

Mansel was invited to deliver the famous Bampton Lectures in the year 1858. The Bamptons were – and are – an annual series, delivered in Oxford, established in the later part of the eighteenth century for the defence of Christian orthodoxy by the late Canon John Bampton. Canon Bampton had a keen grasp of the fallenness of human nature, and particularly of the human nature of which theologians partake, since in his determination to get the lectures published every year he decreed that not only was publication a condition of the appointment of the lecturer, but the fee – a substantial fee – would not be paid until the lectures were in print. It is a comment on the practical wisdom of the man and the truth of the doctrine that in virtually every year of some two hundred, publication has taken place; sometimes, as in the case of Henry Longueville Mansel, in the same year as that in which they were delivered, though we may not say whether in the case of Dean Mansel this should be attributed to a surfeit of the virtue of diligence or of the vice of

5

avarice. To possess them both in good measure would certainly be an advantage in a Bampton Lecturer.

Mansel was a philosopher who wrote on theology and also on church history, but he won particular acclaim amongst his colleagues for his gifts in another direction still, as a writer of humorous verse – the kind of humorous verse which only an Oxford don would write. An excursion into this less arcane area of his work will not, as should later emerge, be altogether without profit. Perhaps its highlight is to be found in his dramatic poem the *Phrontisterion*; which term means a place of learning. Mansel was much concerned about the impact of German philosophy and theology upon Oxford, and the classical chorus to the drama is supplied by a group introduced in the *dramatis personae* as 'Cloudy Professors' from Germany. The chorus make three interventions. First they introduce themselves:

> Professors we,
> From over the sea,
> From the land where Professors in plenty be;
> And we thrive and flourish, as well we may,
> In the land that produced one Kant with a K
> And many Cants with a C.

Then we have this:

> Theologians we,
> Deep thinkers and free,
> From the land of the new Divinity;
> Where Critics hunt for the sense sublime,
> Hidden in texts of the olden time,
> Which none but the sage can see.
> Where Strauss shall teach you how Martyrs died
> For a moral idea personified ....
> Where Feuerbach shows how Religion began
> From the deified feelings and wants of man,
> And the Deity owned by the mind reflective,

6

> Is Human Consciousness made objective.
>   Presbyters, bend,
>   Bishops, attend;
> The Bible's a myth from beginning to end.

And, in their final contribution, as follows – and here in fact we make a beginning – as does Mansel – with the subject which he addresses in his Bampton Lectures, as may be evident:

> The voice of yore,
> Which the breezes bore
> Wailing aloud from Paxo's shore,
> Is changed to a gladder and livelier strain,
> For great God Pan is alive again,
> He lives and reigns once more.

Mansel's Bampton Lectures for 1858 bore the inauspicious title, *The Limits of Religious Thought*, but in this title he has already asked his fundamental question. What are the proper limits to the capacity of man to engage in religious thinking?

Mansel's starting-point is contained in the question, Is the revelation of God open to assessment and evaluation by man? His argument is found in his answer. This can be so only insofar as it is possible for the unaided human reason to construct its own philosophical knowledge of God, apart from his revelation. That is, it is unreasonable to believe these two things at the same time: (1) that a comprehensive knowledge of God is impossible apart from his revelation, and (2) that it is appropriate for the human mind to criticise particular elements within the revelation itself. In Mansel's words,

> If Revelation is a communication from an infinite to a finite intelligence, the conditions of a criticism of Revelation on philosophical grounds must be identical with those which are required for constructing a Philosophy of the Infinite.... Whatever impediments, therefore, exist to prevent the formation of such a

Philosophy, the same impediments must likewise prevent the accomplishment of a complete Criticism of Revelation.[5]

This does not mean that the claims of religion are not open to critical assessment. Mansel's point is that

the legitimate object of a rational criticism of revealed religion, is not to be found in the *contents* of that religion, but in its *evidences*.[6]

The proper task of the mind of man is to decide whether what claims to be a revealed religion *is* a revealed religion. It is not to start sifting through the contents of what it has already decided *is* a revealed religion in an effort to discover whether or not they are true.

Mansel was of course writing in the context of the often naive evidential apologetics of the first half of the English nineteenth century. Whether or not we would place ourselves in the reconstructed evidentialist tradition is not germane to the argument, because all that needs to be meant by the 'evidences' of a religion is the answer that would be given to the question, Why do you believe this religion to be true?

Mansel acknowledges that it is of course possible to regard the 'contents' of a religion as *among* its 'evidences'. But such

---

5. H. L. Mansel, *The Limits of Religious Thought*, London, 1858, pp. 27,8. The *Phrontisterion* will be found in full in H. L. Mansel, *Letters, Lectures and Reviews, including the Phrontisterion*, London, 1873. Mansel's thought is discussed more fully in the present writer's *On the Interpretation of Scripture. Infallibilism and Higher Criticism in Nineteenth-Century Britain* , Lewiston, New York, 1987. His position is applied in a different fashion in 'Universalism and the Logic of Revelation', forthcoming in the *Evangelical Review of Theology*.

6. Mansel, *op. cit.*, p. 234.

scrutiny of 'contents' has as its purpose a decision on whether or not the revelation is genuine. Once scrutiny has taken place a decision must follow for or against. What purports to be a revelation from God either is or is not what it claims. The decision to accept or to reject terminates discussion of the authenticity of the particulars. That is,

> the objections urged against a religion are not like the weights in a scale, which retain their full value, even when outweighed on the other side: – on the contrary, they become absolutely worthless, as soon as we are convinced that there is superior evidence that the religion is true. We may not say, for example, that certain parts of the Christian scheme are unwise or unrighteous, though outweighed by greater acts of righteousness and wisdom: – we are bound to believe that we were mistaken from the first in supposing them to be unwise or unrighteous at all. In a matter of which we are so ignorant and so liable to be deceived, the objection which fails to prove every thing proves nothing: from him that hath not, is taken away even that which he seemeth to have. And on the other hand, an objection which really proves any thing proves every thing. If the teaching of Christ is in any one thing not the teaching of God, it is in all things the teaching of man: its doctrines are subject to all the imperfections inseparable from man's sinfulness and ignorance....[7]

That is to say, the human mind is not equipped to 'divide God's Revelation'. Indeed, Mansel writes,

> Many who would shrink with horror from the idea of rejecting Christ altogether, will yet speak and act as if they were at liberty to set up for themselves an eclectic Christianity.[8]

---

7. *Ibid.*, pp. 246,7.
8. *Ibid.*, pp. 249,50.

And in the phrase 'an eclectic Christianity' we come to the heart of his critique. The claim that we can accept some elements in the Biblical revelation while rejecting others

> rests on a far less reasonable basis than the firm belief which accepts the whole thing, or the complete unbelief that accepts nothing.[9]

That is, 'Rationalism', by which Mansel refers to the eclectic theological method,

> if it retains any portion of revealed truth as such, does so, not in consequence, but in defiance, of its fundamental principle. It does so by virtually declaring that it will follow reason up to a certain point, and no further; though the conclusions which lie beyond that point are guaranteed by precisely the same evidence as those which fall short of it.[10]

Conversely,

> Many a man who rejects isolated portions of Christian doctrine, on the ground that they are repugnant to his reason, would hesitate to avow broadly and unconditionally that reason is the supreme arbiter of all religious truth; though at the same time he would find it hard to point out any particular in which the position of reason, in relation to the truths which he still retains, differs from that which it occupies in relation to those which he rejects.[11]

9.   *Ibid.*, p. 252.
10. *Ibid.*, pp. 10,11.
11. *Ibid.*, p. 1.

THE LOGIC OF BIBLICAL AUTHORITY

Since a 'direct intuition of the infinite is unattainable by human consciousness',[12] the human mind is incompetent to make any such distinctions within the body of revelation itself.

> The conclusion, which an examination of the conditions of human thought unavoidably forces upon us, is this: There can be no such thing as a positive science of Speculative Theology; for such a science must necessarily be based on an apprehension of the Infinite; and the Infinite ... cannot be positively apprehended in any mode of the human Consciousness.... We can test the progress of knowledge, only by comparing its successive representations with the objects which they profess to represent: and as the object in this case is inaccessible to human faculties, we have no criterion [by which to judge.... Such a criterion] can obviously have no place in relation to those truths, if such there be, which human reason is incapable of discovering for itself.[13]

Mansel's analysis of *The Limits of Religious Thought*, the inescapable boundaries of the human mind in its attempt to grapple with religious questions, is an eloquent demonstration of the contention with which we began, that an assault on Biblical authority is less a challenge to particular doctrines than it is to the possibility of Christian doctrine. We turn now to the implications of this thesis for theology, in two distinct conclusions: first in respect of the authoritative role in which the church has always sought to cast Holy Scripture; and, secondly, in respect of our fundamental understanding of the mode of apprehension of God.

---

12. *Ibid.*, p. xxvi, introduction to fourth edition (1859).
13. *Ibid.*, p. 258.

Nigel M. de S. Cameron

Conclusions

1. The Canonicity of Holy Scripture

It is not without interest that the closing chapter of the Bible is devoted in part to this question, in particular, verses 18 and 19. In the *New International Version* they stand as follows:

> I warn everyone who hears the words of the prophecy of this book: If anyone adds anything to them, God will add to him the plagues described in this book. And if anyone takes words away from this book of prophecy, God will take away from him his share in the tree of life and in the holy city, which are described in this book.

It would, of course, be appropriate for us to interpret this text of more than the Revelation to John alone. Its providential placing at the close of the canon of Holy Scripture is an invitation so to do, to treat it as a programmatic statement about the entire volume which, all but for two verses, it closes. But we have no need to argue in this way, since the significance of this statement may be held to lie not in its specific relevance to its context in the Revelation to John, nor in its placing at the end of the canon itself, but as a statement about the role of the Revelation to John as revelation; and, by extension, as a statement about revelation as such.

What these verses say is of course very simple. We are not to add to the book, we are not to take away from it. The man who does either of these things will fall foul of God, whose book it is and whose words it carries. It is a fundamental statement of the canonical principle, and the function of the statement is to assert and safeguard canonical authority.

That is, there are essentially two ways in which the authority of a document can be compromised. It can be added to, and it can be subtracted from. In the case of a substitution of new words for those that are original both subtraction and addition take

12

place simultaneously. Those purposes for which the document has been written will be frustrated if such tampering is effected, because, of course, the upshot of adding words is to place them in the mouth of the author; the upshot of subtracting words is to take them out of his mouth: the net result of either is to subordinate the authority of the author which the document carries to the authority of whosoever has effected the tampering. The author ceases to speak with his own voice, and becomes instead a puppet in the hands of another. It is an exercise in the usurpation of authority.

And it is this which the reader of the Revelation to John the Divine is warned not to do. In one sense, of course, the warning is superfluous. Any authoritative statement carries such a declaration by implication. Without such an implication there could be no such thing as a statement with authority. If addition and subtraction are options for the interpreter then the idea of an authority that can be conveyed in words is void. But there is nothing superfluous about the awesome curses which attend the warning, and it is worth noting that they are said to apply specifically to those who interpret Holy Scripture. A heavy weight of responsibility rests on the shoulders of exegetes, theologians and every expositor of Holy Scripture. We have this document to interpret, but it has been written by another.

Now, it is one of the features of the debate about the Bible that conservatives have found themselves labelled as defenders of many things, and, now, of inerrancy. But that one fundamental doctrine which all our apologetic is intended to support receives hardly a mention: the canonicity of Holy Scripture. Denials of inerrancy matter not because they are denials of inerrancy, but because they are thereby denials at a principial level of canonical authority. The effect of the propaganda which makes out that we are interested only in dotting i's and crossing t's – tithing Bibliological mint and cummin – has been so great that it has even succeeded in convincing *us* – or some of us – that we are fighting in some distant outpost of empire, when it is the motherland of Biblical authority, the church's acceptance of the Bible as canon, which is under attack.

2. *The Incomprehensibility of God*

If the formal victim of the denial of a comprehensive Biblical authority is canonicity, its material concomitant is the incomprehensibility of God. That is to say, the eclectic use of Holy Scripture is logically dependent upon the possibility of what Mansel calls 'Speculative Theology' of 'a Philosophy of the Infinite'; of knowledge of God gained not by revelation, but by the normal, empirical channels whereby we investigate the phenomena of the world of experience.[14] What he calls the 'dividing' of God's revelation can only proceed upon the hidden assumption that revelation is in fact unnecessary; that all that revelation does is to re-publish what we already knew or could have found out for ourselves. Only if all theology is natural theology can the mind of man be given free rein in the evaluation of the contents of the revelation of God.

This point becomes clearer when we use an analogy, a close analogy to which we are actually directed by the verses in Revelation chapter 22 which we have already examined.[15] The writer of Revelation describes the book as a prophecy, and while some of the Biblical books have a particular prophetic character the entire revelation of Holy Scripture may be considered under a prophetic head. Let us suppose we meet a prophet; at least, a man who claims to be a prophet. We weigh up his claims – and there are principles given to us in Scripture to help us in the task. And we come to a conclusion: he is a false prophet, subverting the truth of God, or he is a true prophet, proclaiming it. If we decide that he is speaking on behalf of God, we attend to what he says. We are simply

---

14. The implications of this for the doctrine of eternal punishment are discussed in 'Universalism and the Logic of Revelation', *art.cit.*

15. I am grateful to my friend Dr Peter Jones of Aix-en-Provence for pointing this out with particular clarity.

unable to judge of the veracity of any individual statement as he makes it. Indeed, the significance of his claiming to be a prophet and our recognising him as one lies precisely in this, that he is pretending to authority over us and we are setting ourselves beneath it. It is implied in the nature of the relationship that while we may have competence to recognise a true prophet we do not have competence to weigh his every claim; else, prophet or not, he would not be telling us anything we did not know or could not find out for ourselves by the normal means of enquiry open to us.

That is to say, a claimed competence to judge of the individual elements in a revelation from God entails a competence as broad as the matter of which the revelation treats. Yet such a competence must render the revelation redundant. Only if God is comprehensible to man by nature could the mind of man properly choose to believe *this* of God while rejecting *that*, in exercise of the faculty of critical perception with which the world of man's own immediate experience is assessed.

The challenge to the authority of Holy Scripture should therefore be seen as ultimately destructive of the church's use of Holy Scripture as the canon by which she defines herself, and thereby of her identity as the community founded upon God's self-revelation. An eclectic use of Scripture as authority is only possible upon the assumption – as foreign to the tradition of the church as it is to Holy Scripture – that God may be known without revealing himself, in the same fashion in which we perceive those other objects of our empirical experience. If such were true, of course, it would cease to be significant to speak in terms of revelation, since the logically alternative category of 'discovery', as Kirsopp Lake proposed, would have become the point of departure instead. The notion of a 'revelation' which does no more than state that which can be 'discovered' anyway is one verging on collapse in self-contradiction. Whatever term is employed, God has become by nature comprehensible. He is an empirical object, part of the natural order and the world of common human experience, essentially continuous with and not other than all such objects.

The denial of canonical authority with its concomitant in the implicit denial of the incomprehensibility of God must finally mean the re-establishment of natural religion, that religion which has dogged the footsteps of God's programme of salvation-history from its first beginnings.

Which is why Henry Longueville Mansel so singularly places his finger upon the essence of the new theology in those final lines which we quoted from the *Phrontisterion*. We quote them again:

>   The voice of yore,
>   Which the breezes bore
>   Wailing aloud from Paxo's shore,
> Is changed to a gladder and livelier strain,
> *For great God Pan is alive again,*
> *He lives and reigns once more.*

THE 'ANALOGY OF FAITH' IN THE STUDY OF SCRIPTURE

In Search of Justification and Guide-lines

HENRI BLOCHER

Analogia fidei – the Reformers and their spiritual seed in the sixteenth and seventeenth centuries embroidered in gold thread upon their banners the apostle Paul's somewhat enigmatic phrase (Rom.12:6). These words signified for them the 'basic rule' of their hermeneutics, the *'principium seu fundamentum interpretationis'*.[1] The analogy of faith helped them to clothe the rather abstract maxim, 'Scripture, its own interpreter', with exegetical flesh; that is, it suggested what kind of procedures the maxim could entail; only thus could promoters of the *'sola Scriptura'* silence Roman Catholic controversialists. It has fallen, however, into remarkable neglect on the part of contemporary theologians, though they glory so candidly in their enlightened hermeneutical consciousness. In recent years, only a few Evangelicals have called attention back to the analogy of faith: Robert C. Sproul has given a quick but useful overview of the theme;[2] Walter C. Kaiser, with characteristic intrepidity, has offered some new insights;[3] finally, his Trinity colleague Donald A. Carson, who knows how happily to combine scientific exegesis with dogmatic responsibility, has made a perceptive contribution, with systematic theology, *ex*

---

1. Max-Albrecht Landerer, 'Hermeneutik', in Herzog's *Real-Encyklopädie für protestantische Theologie und Kirche,* Stuttgart & Hamburg, 1856, V, 783.
2. 'Biblical Interpretation and the Analogy of Faith', in Roger R. Nicole & J. Ramsay Michaels, ed., *Inerrancy and Common Sense,* Grand Rapids, 1980, pp. 119-135.
3. *Toward an Exegetical Theology. Biblical Exegesis for Preaching and Teaching,* Grand Rapids, 1981, esp. pp. 82ff, 94, 133ff, 145, 161. Kaiser quotes from John J. Johnson, *'Analogia fidei* as Hermeneutical Principle', *Springfielder,* 36, 1972-73, pp.249-259.

professo, in view .[4]   It is high time that those who labour in the systematic field should rally and consider re-appropriating a not insignificant part of their heritage.

Exploration

All church doctors who appealed to the 'analogy of faith' did not understand exactly the same thing, even among the Protestant orthodox.   Lucidity requires that various conceptions be disentangled from each other, and their historical connections be brought to light.

The older, pre-Reformation, focus had been on the substance of revealed truth, as taught by the Church.   This was the norm;[5] it had been regarded *ex hypothesi* as the authentic content of Scripture, often summed up in the Apostles' Creed.   The emphasis had shifted from the guarantee offered by the mother-churches of apostolic sees to the unanimous consent of the Fathers, the decrees of the ecumenical councils, and formal recognition by the magisterium.   This first understanding did

---

4.   'Unity and Diversity in the New Testament: The Possibility of Systematic Theology', in D.A. Carson & J.D. Woodbridge, ed., *Scripture and Truth,* Grand Rapids, 1983, pp. 65-95, esp. 90ff. Carson mentions Daniel P. Fuller, 'Biblical Theology and the Analogy of Faith', in *Unity and Diversity in New Testament Theology,* Robert E. Guelich, ed., Grand Rapids, 1978, pp. 195-213, and Robert L. Thomas, 'A Hermeneutical Ambiguity of Eschatology: The Analogy of Faith', *Journal of the Evangelical Theological Society* 23, 1980, pp.45-53.   We had no access either to Johnson's or to these articles.

5.   The phrase 'analogy of faith', is not at all usual in Patristic and medieval writings;   rather the norm bears many names: the faith, the catholic faith, the rule of truth, the preaching, the (order of) tradition, the measure of faith (*mensura fidei,* Victorinus of Pettau), all of these 'apostolic' or 'ecclesiastical', and even 'the ancient institution of the Church'*(archaion tês ekklêsias sustêma,* Irenaeus).   But Romans 12:6 was often interpreted in terms of conformity precisely with that norm (mostly among Latin Fathers).

not disappear from Protestant ranks. Reformed divines, especially, echo traditional statements and often consider the agreement with the Apostolicum as the basic meaning (*Inbegriff*) of the analogy of faith.[6] Georg Sohnius, a Professor at Heidelberg c. 1585, could write:

> The norm and rule of this interpretation is faith and love: faith is expounded in the symbol of the apostles, love in the Decalogue. Hence, the apostle prescribes that interpretation be analogous to faith (Rom.12:6), that is, that it should agree with the first axioms or principles, so to speak, of faith, as well as with the whole body of heavenly doctrine.[7]

Many others would adopt a similar stance.[8] Peter Martyr even granted a second rank authority to 'the constant consent and verdict of the church'.[9] We would call the first version of the *analogia fidei* the 'traditional' one.

Luther originated a second type. His explosive experience of liberation by the Word of God centred upon a limited number of particular verses: these *helle und kläre Worte*, 'clear, luminous, words', had conquered his soul, and almost became to him, as our venerated friend, the late Richard Stauffer, once said in a

---

6. Otto Ritschl, *Dogmengeschichte des Protestantismus*, Leipzig, 1908, vol.I, p. 357.
7. 'Norma et regula hujus interpretationis est fides et caritas: quarum illa in symbolo apostolorum, haec in decalogo exponitur. Unde apostolus praecipit ut interpretatio sit analogia fidei, Rom. cap.12, hoc est, cum primis fidei axiomatis et quasi principiis totoque coelestis doctrinae corpore consentiat', *De Verbo Dei*, as quoted *ibid.*
8. Cf. Heinrich Heppe, *Die Dogmatik der evangelische-reformierten Kirche*, Ernst Bizer, ed., Neukirchen, 1935, p.13, quoting, e.g., Chamier: *'Analogia fidei* est argumentatio a generalibus, quae omnium in ecclesia docendorum normam continet'.
9. 'Consensus auctoritasque constans ecclesiae', *ibid.*, p. 29.

pleasant mood, his 'fetish texts'.[10]   Among these were
Hannah's song of the Lord as bringing death and making alive
(1 Sam.2:6), Isaiah's enigmatic oracle on the Lord's 'strange'
work (Is.28:21), the institution of the Lord's Supper (so plain
that the effort of the Swiss to find there some kind of figurative
language passed his comprehension and showed a perverse
mind, another Spirit), Paul's principle of every man a liar, in
front of God the only truthful (Rom.3:4), and, of course, the
paradox of justification by faith alone, without works....
Interpreting Scripture according to the analogy of faith meant
following the lead and light of the clearer passages.   Their
power to illuminate conferred on them the regulative function.
Here Luther's dramatic experience converged with a common-
sense recommendation, and the emphasis on the privilege of
clearer passages has remained strong among Lutherans and
other Protestants.   J. Gerhard can define the norm as the 'sum
of heavenly doctrine gathered from the most 'open' places of
Scripture'.[11] Chemnitz requires agreement with the points 'that
have express, clear, sure, and firm witness in the Scripture'.[12]
On the Reformed side, Herman Bavinck states that the original
view (that of his theological forefathers) stressed the sense
drawn from clear verses.[13]   Significantly, the treatment of the
analogy of faith belongs to the section on the 'perspicuity' of
Scripture.

---

10. In a private lecture to a small group, to which the present writer
     belonged, in Paris, 27 Oct. 1977. Otto Ritschl, *op.cit.,* has
     shown the decisive role which the *helle und kläre Worte* played.
11. 'Summa quaedam coelestis doctrinae ex apertissimis scripturae
     locis collecta', quoted by Landerer, 783.
12. Quoted by Robert D. Preus, *The Theology of Post-Reformation
     Lutheranism. A Study of Theological Prolegomena,* Saint Louis
     and London, 1970, p. 97.
13. 'Uit de duidelijke plaatsen', *Gereformeerde Dogmatiek* , Kampen,
     1906[2], I, p.511.   On the same page he refers to Voetius and
     Turretin.

THE ANALOGY OF FAITH

After the 'topically selective' version comes the 'thematically selective' one. The third understanding of the *analogia fidei* may also claim Luther as its father. Conformity prevails with a cardinal truth of revelation, with a central theological principle taken as the key to all the rest. In his major attack upon the views of the *Schwarmgeister* or sacramentarians of Zurich and Basel, *On the Supper of Christ. Confession* (1528), Luther complains that their exegesis of the words of institution spoils them of their usefulness, 'and this, all the more, since there is no *analogia fidei* here. For all the words of Christ must bear faith and love and be analogous to faith, Romans 12'.[14] Luther probably means that the figurative interpretation suppresses the need for faith exercised against sight, does not set the truth of God against every man a liar, is not analogous to the justification of the wicked and to Christology, which turns upside down the judgement of the senses and of reason. Melanchthon joins this view of the analogy with the traditional understanding when he asks for congruence 'with the foundation, that is the law, and the gospel, and the symbols'.[15] Calvin's dedicatory epistle to King Francis I, with which he prefaced the *Institutes*, magnificently expounds the *soli Deo gloria* as the normative reference for the analogy of faith:

> When Saint Paul decided that all prophecy should conform to the analogy and similitude of faith (Rom.12:6), he set a most certain rule to test every interpretation of Scripture. If our doctrine is examined by this rule of faith, victory is ours. What better agrees with faith than our acknowledging ourselves to be naked of all virtue, to be clothed upon by God? Void of all good, to be filled by him? Slaves of sin, to be freed by

---

14. After the French translation by Jean Bosc, *Martin Luther, Oeuvres*, vol.VI (Geneva, 1964) p. 93 = *Weimar Ausgabe* vol.26, p.390.
15. 'Et in primis teneamus regulam, ut prophetia sit analoga fidei, id est, ut enarrationes et judicia congruant cum fundamento, id est cum lege et evangelio et symbolis', *Corpus Reform*. 15, col.1008, as quoted by Ritschl, p. 302.

him? Blind, to be given light of him? Lame, to be straightened by him? Feeble, to be of him sustained? To deprive ourselves of all matter of boasting that he alone may be glorified, and we in him?[16]

Amandus Polanus (1561-1610) offers a more scholastic but no less trenchant formulation of the same criterion:

> This interpretation agrees with Holy Scripture which attributes to God all the praise of our eternal salvation, and, at the same time, takes it away entirely from man; that one does not truly agree with Holy Scripture which ascribes to man any, or the smallest, part of the glory of eternal salvation.[17]

Nothing could be more congenial to the Barthian mind: the Christological 'concentration', the triumph of grace, the 'Jesus is Victor' central proclamation, govern the whole Barthian enterprise. It is Barth who revives the memory of Polanus,

---

16. After the French original, *Institution de la Religion chrétienne* (Geneva, 1955) I, p. xxiv: 'Quand saint Paul a voulu que toute prophétie fût conforme à l'analogie et similitude de la foi (Rom.12:6), il a mis une très certaine règle pour éprouver toute interprétation de l'Ecriture. Or si notre doctrine est examinée à cette règle de foi, nous avons la victoire en main. Car quelle chose convient mieux à la foi, que de nous reconnaître nus de toute vertu pour être vêtus de Dieu? vides de tout bien, pour être emplis de lui? serfs de péché, pour être délivrés de lui? aveugles, pour être de lui illuminés? boîteux, pour être de lui redressés? débiles, pour être de lui soutenus? de nous ôter toute matière de gloire, afin que lui seul soit glorifié, et nous en lui?' In the *Institutes* itself Calvin refers twice to the analogy as a theological principle, 4:16:4 and 4:17:32 (less clear).

17. 'Illa autem (interpretatio) consentit cum sacra scriptura, quae omnem laudem salutis nostrae aeternae in solidum Deo tribuit et homini prorsus adimit: illa vero non consentit cum sacra scriptura, quaecunque vel minimam partem gloriae salutis aeternae homini adscribit', *Syntagma Theologiae christianae*, as quoted by K. Barth, *Church Dogmatics*, I, 2, sect. 21/2, under point 2.

although his own use of the phrase itself, *analogia fidei*, has more to do with the cognitive value of religious language, or 'God-talk'.[18] It is Thomas F. Torrance who refers us back to Calvin's preface, with obvious pleasure and assurance.[19]

A majority of Protestants, over the centuries, have probably subscribed to a fourth version. We could describe it as the more 'formal' one, *analogia totius Scripturae*. The main application of the analogy is the comparison of all relevant passages on any topic, under the methodical duty to avoid substantial contradictions. It implies a systematic character in biblical interpretation, the totality of a coherent Scripture being the norm. One is not far from the older idea of the 'hermeneutical circle', the reciprocal determination of the whole and of the parts. Thus the *Second Helvetic Confession* ask that Scripture be expounded 'according to the comparison of similar or dissimilar passages'.[20] Hollaz defines the analogy of faith as 'the harmony of biblical statements'.[21] For Abraham Kuyper, as the last essential hermeneutical rule, it amounts to taking seriously the oneness of the biblical corpus.[22] Even Pope Leo XIII in his encyclical *Providentissimus Deus* (1893)

---

18. The *analogia fidei* is for Barth the alternative to the *analogia entis*, not a rule for hermeneutics, but the way to relate our words to Divine reality. The fullest discussion is found in the *Church Dogmatics* II, 1, sect. 27/2, point 3, where he also coins the phrase *analogia gratiae*, and agrees to define it as an *analogia attributionis extrinsecae*. In I, 12, section 1/2, the analogy of faith is nearer to functioning as a criterion of theological work.
19. *Theological Science*, Oxford, London, New York, 1969, pp. x, 244f.
20. Ch.II: 'pro ratione locorum vel similium vel dissimilium'. This is one element only in a mixed conception.
21. 'Harmonia dictorum biblicorum', in Landerer, 783.
22. *Encyclopaedie der Heilige Godgeleerdheid*, Amsterdam, 1894, vol.III, p. 106.

seems to use *analogia fidei* with regard to the non-contradictory character of Scripture.[23]

We shall raise the question, first, of the meaning of the phrase in the verse from which it was extracted, and which was used to enhance the authority of the rule; then, of the logical mapping of the views we have sketched, whether they include, exclude, or complement one another. A theological justification should come afterwards, of the version, pure or mixed, which will attract our preference, and guide-lines for practice.

Confrontation

Modern commentators of Paul's injunction in Romans 12:6 often appear quite sure that the apostle means 'faith' in the subjective sense, *fides qua* (so F.F. Bruce, John Murray, C.E.B. Cranfield, to choose scholars worthy of the highest consideration); in that case, there is little connection between that verse and the theologians' *analogia fidei* throughout church history. Paul either encouraged would-be prophets in the church to exercise their gifts when they felt confident of having received a message, or he exhorted them to purify their motives or attitudes and only to speak in conformity with their subjective faith, that is, in sober recognition of their dependence on Christ. Unexpected help, however, has come to the Latin Fathers' and Calvin's side! Ernst Käsemann argues forcefully in favour of an objective sense of 'faith': 'It makes no sense at all to suggest that the prophet must judge himself by his own faith.... This would open the gates to every abuse and even false

---

23. It is reproduced in F. Vigouroux, ed., *Dictionnaire de la Bible*, vol.I, Paris, 1909, and reads on p. xxii: 'Analogia fidei sequenda est, et doctrina catholica ...', adding: 'ex quo apparet, eam interpretationem ut ineptam et falsam rejiciendam, quae, vel inspiratos auctores inter se quodammodo pugnantes faciat, vel doctrinae ecclesiae adversatur'. In the correspondence between the two sentences, to the *analogia fidei* answers the rejection of any interpretation which would create a conflict between inspired writers of the Bible.

teaching'.[24]   Alphonse Maillot follows him.[25]   Heinrich
Schlier reaches a similar conclusion.[26] We may surely surmise
that a subjective criterion would generate more problems than it
would solve.   'Faith' in the objective sense occurs not so
seldom in Paul's writings (in Gal.1:23; 3:23,25; 6:10, to take an
early epistle, *pistis* refers to the message, or regime, or bond of
fellowship; also probably in Eph.4:5,13; 1 Tim.2:7; 3:9; 4:1,6;
5:8; 6:10,12,21; 2 Tim.3:8 ;4:7; Tit.1:1; possibly in Rom.1:5;
10:8; 16:26; Col.2:7; 1 Tim.1:19; Tit.1:4, 13 ;3:15).   Long
before the Pastoral Epistles Paul expressed the idea of a 'model'
or 'pattern' of doctrine (Rom.6:17), and if he meant the same
under 'faith', he could easily combine the word *analogia* with it.
When prophecy is the topic under discussion, the New
Testament quite regularly stresses the need for discernment (1
Cor.14:29,37f; 1 Thes.5:20f; 1 Pet.4:11; 1 Jn.4:1-6), and
whenever the criterion is explicitly stated or hinted at, it is
conformity with apostolic teaching, with *fides quae creditur*.
We dare even suggest that the 'measure of faith' of Romans
12:3 could be interpreted along the same lines.   According to
the primary meaning of the word, the 'measure' is the
measuring measure, the standard;[27]   may we not understand
that God has allotted to each Christian his function in the body
in harmony with (accusative of reference) the standard of the
new regime of faith, otherwise called 'the measuring standard of
the gift of Christ' (Eph.4:7)?   Such an exegesis would confirm
Käsemann's in verse 6:   the apostle instructs his readers that
prophecy should agree with the message and doctrine they have
received.   If New Testament church prophecy, as solid studies

---

24. *Commentary on Romans,* tr. by G.W. Bromiley, London, p. 341.
     Apart from Bultmann, he mentions E. Schweizer and W. Schrage
     on the same side.
25. *L'épître aux Romains, épître de l'oecuménisme et théologie de
     l'histoire,* Paris, et Geneva, 1984, pp. 306f.
26. *Der Römerbrief,* Freiburg, Basel, Vienna, Herder, 1977, p. 370.
27. As C.E.B. Cranfield, *A Critical and Exegetical Commentary on
     the Epistle to the Romans,* Edinburgh, 1979, vol.II, p. 615, has
     well perceived and warranted.   The Peshitta uses the same word
     for *metron* and *analogia* in verses 3 and 6.

indicate, covered a wide range of forms, and was closely bound with the exposition of Scripture,[28] later appeals to the analogy of faith may not be altogether foreign to the original meaning of Romans 12:6.

We are not, however, to put all conceptions on the same footing. The four main types briefly characterized above are neither equivalent nor mutually exclusive. If one seeks a consensus with every part of Scripture (version IV), he will *ipso facto* honour the central thrust of its message (version III) – provided the Bible *is* coherent – and find support in the clearest places (version II); the risks are not too frightening, then, of a denial of the Creed (version I). Yet, the converse is not true. Karl Barth can both claim conformity with the Word of God, to which Scripture witnesses, and reject Hollaz' rule, harmonization with all biblical statements. The Roman Catholic form of the 'traditional' conception is incompatible with the Reformation principle; while the Fathers and medieval doctors avoided making a decision. They confessed the supreme authority of Holy Scripture but never conceived of it as a tool for the critique of the Church. We cannot elude the choice. What are we to retain, and what are we to reject, if we wish helpfully to use the words *analogia fidei*, and so name a rule for our own Bible study and theologizing?

Courage sometimes requires a degree of bluntness. No church, we dare assert, can faithfully render to its Lord his due of honour and obedience which forbids the Lord's Word radically to question and redress all of its ways and all of its thoughts. We concur with the following admonition:

> What happens when a corporate body lacking a clear external standard of truth and judgement grows in strength?... The corporate body strives to become a

---

28. Strongly asserted by E. Cothenet, 'Prophétisme dans le Nouveau Testament', in *Supplément au Dictionnaire de la Bible*, vol. VII, Paris, 1972, cols. 1280, 1299f.

> standard to itself, a law to itself. In a word, it presses forward to the status of a Leviathan, that 'mortal god' which Hobbes described so accurately. (....) In sum: unless an infallible, inerrant Word stands above the church, judging it and proclaiming grace to it, magisterial authority is the greatest liability the church can have, for it will inevitably become the unprincipled tool and demonic reflection of sinful man.[29]

In principle, therefore, no ecclesiastical interpretation or summary of the faith may be allowed to govern the reading of Scripture, and thus to encroach on the free exercise of the Lord's sovereignty over his own through the Word. The privilege of the clearer passages may appear, in the second version, as harmless enough. But who will tell which verses are clear and which are not? Who shall declare the 'obvious' meaning? Historical experience warns against naïve optimism here. Luther's own example, on the eucharistic words of Jesus, will to many appear more repulsive than attractive. Subjectivism inevitably attaches itself to the selection of some elements in a class, to be made the key to all the rest, if it is the first step in a method. The same defect mars, and even more seriously, the other 'selective' version of the analogy of faith. Elevating to a superior normative status one particular doctrine cannot be done without facing the charge of arbitrariness: lack of control makes it too easy for personal preference or philosophical influence to interfere. If one claims that the Spirit so leads (or that the object of the witness imposes himself), he

29. John Warwick Montgomery, *Ecumenicity, Evangelicals, and Rome*, Grand Rapids, 1969, pp. 40f. The Chapter was previously published as an article in the *Springfielder*.

falls back into the old illuministic trap.[30] Karl Barth himself was never able to show how to resist the temptation. Only with the formal-universal analogy of faith and Scripture do we stand on less slippery ground. Like every other rule, it may be misapplied, but, within its frame, constitutional provision is made for correction by an objective standard. This is unique. In principle, no Scriptural evidence, in whatsoever way it may bear upon an issue, will be denied the right to overthrow preconceived ideas and slanted approaches. Once it is accepted, adequate room can be made for the interests represented in the other views. Under the safeguard of a prior commitment to comply with all inspired pronouncements, one can happily look for the axis of revelation, as Calvin did, and gather light from *helle und kläre Worte* as they appear to shine, and pay due respect to the ministerial authority of the church, with its *normae normatae*. These prove themselves to be precious heuristic procedures. We would recommend a complex notion of the *analogia fidei*, with the formal-universal version as the basis, and secondary features added from the other three.

The apostle, when dictating Romans 12:6, barely thought of the technical 'comparing Scripture with Scripture'; yet, he concerned himself with the agreement of Christian discourse with the whole body of teaching given by inspiration of God, in its main emphases and overall balance *(analogia)*, all parts included. Substantially, his point was not far removed from our suggested conception of the analogy of faith. We may recall this nearness to accredit the rule, but, in order to confirm it, a broader theological justification would not be superfluous.

---

30. James I. Packer, 'Infallible Scripture and the Role of Hermeneutics', in *Scripture and Truth, op. cit.*, p. 347, uses exceptionally strong language for 'the regular neoorthodox appeal to the Spirit as interpreter': 'an appeal that appears on analysis to be an illuminist fig leaf donned to conceal disfiguring incoherence and arbitrariness in handling the text'. At p.350, he commends the Reformers' *analogia Scripturae*, which he himself calls the principle of harmony.

THE ANALOGY OF FAITH

Justification

The analogy of faith, as we understand it, rests first and foremost on the ground of *biblical coherence*. It retains its normative force if, and only if, Scripture is consistent with itself, that is, if all its affirmations are consonant with one another in their original, authentic meaning. Not all scholars wish to grant the truth of this proposition. Many, even before negating the doctrinal consistency of Scripture *in fact*, deny that Scripture *claims* such an attribute, or that formal coherence better suits its function and is more congruous with divinity than the blissful inconsistencies of life.[31]   Ever-changing life! Cannot the God of life and of paradoxical *kenosis*, the God who writes straight on crooked lines and takes pleasure in always surprising us, speak through contradictions?   The opposite, traditional, opinion is charged with Western, or Greek, or Cartesian, 'rationalism'!

On the rock unmoved, he who coolly examines the data sees through contemporary rhetoric.   At all stages of biblical history, coherence is highly valued, and ascribed to whatever teaching is believed to have come from God.   Truth, *emeth* , rhymes with eternity, immutable permanence (Ps.119:160, etc.).[32]   The law of the Lord is pure, that is, perfectly homogeneous, more thoroughly purged of dross than refined silver and gold; all his ordinances go together as one in their rightness (Ps.19:9).   No miracle may authorize unorthodox prophecies (Dt.13:1ff).   In

---

31. For a forceful plea of that kind, see Louis Simon, 'Le Scandale et l'unite' in *Parole et dogmatique. Hommage a Jean Bosc,* 1971, pp. 226-231, and the special issue of the Dominican review *Lumiere et Vie* , Lyons, 20/103, June-July 1971, 'Unity and Conflicts in the Church', especially the contributions by E. Trocme and L. Dewart.

32. Cf. Roger Nicole, 'The Biblical Concept of Truth', In *Scripture and Truth, op. cit.,* pp. 287-298, notes 410f.   One may consult our study, 'Qu'est-ce que la vérité?   Orientations bibliques dans le débat', *Hokhma* 12, 1979, pp.2-13 and 13, 1980, pp.38-49.

spite of God's freedom to display new things in history, failure to harmonize with the dominant tone of earlier revelations raises doubts on the authenticity of a message (Je.28:7ff). Paul exhorts his readers to be of one mind (Phil.2:2, etc.); they are to grow into the unity of faith (Eph.3:13), since there is only, under one Lord, one faith and one baptism (v.5). His preaching is not 'Yes' and 'No' (2 Cor. 1:18), an echo of Jesus' famous words. In contrast, Friedrich Engels once commented that saying 'Yes, yes, and no, no', is doing 'metaphysics', a capital sin, indeed, in his eyes![33] Paul insists that his message is identical with that of the other apostles (1 Cor.15:11); their approval and recognition gave him the assurance that he was not running in vain (Gal.2:2). In the face of misinterpretations, 2 Peter 3:16 reaffirms this accord. John highlights the three witnesses' agreement (1 Jn.5:8), and the Fourth Gospel puts forward the theme of 'repetition', not parrot-like indeed, but meeting a concern for identity of substance (Jn.8:26,28; 16:13). Discord is a symptom of untruth, as it was in the case of the false witnesses of Jesus' trial (Mk.14:56,59). Contradictors are to be refuted (Rom.16:17; Tit.1:9): it could never be done if the standard itself embraced several conflicting theologies. As a matter of fact, the whole logic of our Lord's appeal to Scripture in argument (and similarly of his apostles') would instantly collapse if the presupposition of scriptural coherence were taken away. Even against the Tempter, Jesus relies on the internal consistency of his Father's Word, quoting Scripture to rebuff a twisted use of Scripture. 'It is written' would no longer settle an issue if it were conceded that several contradictory views compete with each other on the pages of the Book. The authority of the Word of God would no longer function as it does in Scripture in that case (how could it function at all as supreme?). The men of God who had a part in writing the

---

33. According to the great marxist thinker Lucien Goldmann, *Le Dieu caché*, Paris, 1955, p. 187.

Bible prized consistency;[34] they ascribed it axiomatically to divine revelation; it belonged to the collection of sacred texts which had been handed down to them and was enlarged through their own ministry.

Was the latter conviction well-founded? This is another matter. It is possible to imagine that they were actually deluded, and our Lord with them, the victims of their cultural assumptions, and could not see the real inconsistencies in the texts. The size of this paper forbids that we should try to give any proof, even minimal, of our conclusion to the contrary. We shall take shelter behind the refutation of Bauer's and Käsemann's views by D.A. Carson or I. Howard Marshall,[35] and limit ourselves to a couple of remarks. Scholarly research on the phenomena, first, provided it is not swayed by presuppositions alien from the Christian faith or hostile to it, provided it is oriented by the Christian worldview, does see and show the harmony of biblical statements. Difficulties which have plagued former generations of readers have been solved wonderfully; those that remain are seldom very acute and are fewer in number than we could reasonably expect – when we think of the *lacunae* in what we know about context and circumstances, about language and literary conventions. Likewise, theological reflection does perceive, with awesome delight, the symphonic beauty of revealed truth. Without becoming masters of God's mysteries, still seeing in part, *en ainigmati*, we do catch a glimpse of a

---

34. The opposite is so unnatural that those modern critics who deny ancient Israelites 'our' sense of coherence and so explain that they were able to sew together contradictory doublets, etc., still divide among sources in view of supposed inconsistencies incompatible with oneness of source: the original writer (a Cartesian mind indeed!) cannot have written both *a* and *b*, hence they must come from two different documents *A* and *B* ....

35. D.A. Carson, *op.cit.*, and I.H. Marshall, 'Orthodoxy and Heresy in Earlier Christianity', *Themelios*, 2/1, 1976-77, p.5-14. Cf. also Harald Riesenfeld, *Unité et diversité dans le Nouveau Testament,* tr. into French by L-M. Dewailly, *Lectio divina* 98, Paris, Cerf, 1979.

glorious coherence, we do enjoy the earnest of vision. The second remark recalls the status and modality of our profession: it is *of faith*. If we walked by sight, if we followed exclusively our apprehension of the phenomena, problems still on our hands would prevent us from affirming a *perfect* consistency of all the parts of Scripture. But we rather believe our Lord than our eyes. We follow him in his attitude towards the Word of God written – are there other ways of *consistent* discipleship? Whatever be the depths of God's condescension and accommodation to our weakness, we have his word that human agency did not mix alien opinions with the purity of divine truth: we may, therefore, resort with full assurance of faith to the *analogia fidei*.

While scriptural coherence is the foundational justification of the analogy of faith, it requires a second condition to be truly functional: the validity of *canonical enclosure*. The discipline of harmony needs a well-defined corpus within the bounds of which it can operate. Such a prerequisite is implicit in the first one, since, without it, 'Scripture' and 'scriptural' would lose their precise reference; but it is better to spell it out, although more than a mere mention is hardly possible here. Suffice it to say that biblical evidence does warrant the principle of canon. Our Lord endorsed the canonical discernment (well-nigh achieved at that time) of official Judaism. In spite of his critical bent, a major scholar like Hans von Campenhausen acknowledges in the apostle Paul 'the first theologian of a new Canon, based on the history of Christ', what we call the New Testament.[36] The rise and flourishing of 'canonical criticism' in the last fifteen years, shows a new and welcome sensitivity to the blessing of canon, despite shortcomings as regards the *locus* of authority. Brevard S. Childs, the gifted leader who launched the movement in 1970, will not submit to a strict analogy of faith; in actual practice, Child's (hypothetical)

---

36. *La Formation de la Bible Chrétienne*, tr. into French by Denise Appia & Max Dominice, Neuchâtel-Paris, 1971, p. 113. He has in mind especially 1 Cor. 11 and 15.

reconstruction of editorial selection and changes, redactional work and re-casting of material by so-called 'canonizers', has more import than the final form of the text;[37] nevertheless, his partial re-discovery of biblical unity has opened the way to unusually wholesome interpretation, at least in several cases.[38] From the standpoint of biblical theology, Meredith G. Kline's original and convincing work has unearthed the foundation of the canonical institution, a development of the covenant treaty document.[39] We may also comment that the neat canonical boundary which sets apart the Word of God among human writings is a sign of God's real involvement in history: his Word comes down to earth without ceasing to be his Word.

The analogy of faith also depends, at least for its usefulness, on the *organic and natural character* of biblical discourse. This condition has been somewhat ignored, except one takes it as implicit in the *external perspicuity* of orthodox divines.[40] Yet, it fully deserves our attention. If Scripture were a collection of independent sayings, all of them right but simply juxtaposed, on topics unconnected with one another, how could the analogy come into play? In the case of a systematic treatise, with each point dealt with once, in logical order, comparison of passages would be of secondary interest. But Scripture, like ordinary speech and even more so, shows much repetition and redundancy, it mixes freely general and particular statements, it incorporates dialogue and much figurative language, it multiplies cross-references: the very situation in which analogical interpretation is most needed and most fruitful. It

---

37. On the canonical approach, we recommend the special issue of the *Journal for the Study of the Old Testament* 16, 1980. James Barr's critique is just as fierce as could be expected; yet, from the opposite pole, we would agree with many of his strictures on Childs' equivocations or compromises.
38. E.g., his treatment of Ps. 8 in his first 'canonical 'work, *Biblical Theology in Crisis,* Philadelphia, 1970, pp. 151-163.
39. *The Structure of Biblical Authority*, Grand Rapids, 1972; first articles in the *Westminster Theological Journal.*
40. Landerer, 783.

justifies the search for the clearer words. Furthermore, biblical diversity resembles that of a living organism: some truths are more vital than others (Mt.23:23), a supreme common aim determines the general direction, that God be glorified (cf.Jn.7:18), Jesus Christ himself being the head of that body of truth (2 Cor.1:20, etc.). This is proper ground for giving a major (not exclusive) role to major doctrinal themes and patterns. Interpretation according to the analogy of faith, with its various components, espouses Scripture as it is!

A *caveat*, however, comes from the ardent Old Testament scholar, Walter C. Kaiser: if the analogy of faith were to rule interpretation, he fears, with later doctrines used as exegetical keys, 'all revelation would then be levelled out'.[41] The analogy of *antecedent* Scripture alone has legitimacy in the study of Scripture.[42] Kaiser's praiseworthy concern focuses on the human author's mind, which we ought not to by-pass, as God was pleased to bind himself to it: the mystery of inspiration is the creation of God of his own meaning *as* the meaning of the man, and we would destroy the mystery if we were to read into the words another meaning than the man's.[43] Now, obviously, a given sacred writer could only know what was revealed prior to his own ministry, 'antecedent Scripture'. This is the only context we may take into account. Carson's cautious reply - 'that would mean no really new revelation could ever be admitted'[44] - seems to hit beyond the mark; for, on Kaiser's premises, an entirely new item of revelation *may* be introduced: simply, the analogy of antecedent Scripture will

---

41. *Toward an Exegetical Theology*, p. 161.
42. *Ibid.*, p. 90.
43. James I. Packer, 'Preaching as Biblical Interpretation', in *Inerrancy and Common Sense, op. cit.*, p. 198, stresses: 'The whole point of the doctrine of inspiration' amounts to this, 'the way into God's mind is via the human authors' expressed meaning'; and he adds, p. 199: 'The basic theological significance in calling Scripture "inerrant" is as an avowal of this identity'.
44. 'Unity and Diversity ...', p. 92.

afford no help for its interpretation,[45] and only the other (philological) rules will then govern exegesis. However, we also demur at Kaiser's exclusion of the analogy of faith; we would not lightheartedly relinquish assistance from posterior Scripture! Kaiser apparently overlooks an interesting fact: the identity of the prophet's (or psalmist's, etc.) mind and of the mind of the Spirit cuts both ways. With any one human writer, we do admit that later statements clarify earlier ones; if we can trust, at least, the continuity of his thought, later expressions shed hermeneutical light on preceding ones, and they dispel misunderstandings. Why should not later expressions of the unchanging mind of the Spirit, spoken through holy men of God, clarify the meaning of older inspired words? If the meaning of the prophet and that of the Spirit coincide, better to ascertain the mind of the Spirit *is* better to ascertain the mind of the prophet. This involves no forcing of additional *content*, drawn, e.g., from the Gospels, into Isaiah's words; later revelation provides us with *contextual* information in the widest sense, a significant hermeneutical help in correcting mistakes. Critics who do not acknowledge the role of the Spirit as *auctor primarius* may look down on our procedures as 'unscientific', but we have not received a spirit of timidity! We are also aware of the pitfalls: an accurate evaluation of the bearing of later statements on a given debate of interpretation demands much skill, caution and tactfulness. But, in consequence, let us not renounce the *analogia fidei:* let us make a better use of it!

Directions

Examining Walter C. Kaiser's objections and proposals has already led us into our last area of study, on the practical level of actual use. *How* should we apply the analogy of faith? Are there guide-lines to follow? Abraham Kuyper, while fervently

---

45. It will still exercise a negative control: absence of contradiction with prior revelation will allow the acceptance of a new item, if the new revelation can show the proper credentials (signs, etc.).

upholding the principle, voices concerns not so far from
Kaiser's:

> The whole of Scripture was considered too much as a
> text-book written *aus einem Guss* (at a stretch), and the
> *historia revelationis* constituted too little the complement
> of serious study.   By so doing one would confuse
> analogy and identity. (...) One would thus pay too little
> attention to the distinction between the essence and the
> form of revelation, and not understand how, also apart
> from the historical process, the same essence can reveal
> itself in a plurality of forms, just as a shaft of light is
> broken into a plurality of colours through a prism.
> Finally, one would overlook that the content of
> revelation as proceeding from God was too rich to be
> enclosed in one form only.[46]

He complains that the *analogia fidei* was reduced to 'mechanical
stiffness and rigidity';   it is 'no identical repetition', but should
be 'governed by the organic process of revelation which also
requires it'.[47] We might question Kuyper's antithesis between
analogy and identity as somewhat facile (since neither in
Romans 12:6 nor with the Reformers is the concept thus

---

46. 'Geheel de Schrift werd te zeer als een *aus einem Guss* geschreven
Tekstboek beschouwd, en de historia revelationis vormde te
weinig voorwerp van ernstige studie.   Analogie werd zoodoende
verward met identiteit.   (...)   Evenzoo had men te weinig oog
voor de distinctie tusschen wezen en vorm der Openbaring, en
begreep niet, hoe, ook buiten het historisch proces, hetzelfde
wezen zich in veelheid van vormen kon openbaren, gelijk de
lichtstraal door de lijnen van het prisma zich in een veelheid van
kleuren oplost.   En eindelijk zag men voorbij, dat hetgeen te
openbaren was uit God kwam, en daarom te rijk aan inhoud was,
om zich in één enkelen vorm op te sluiten', *Encyclopaedie* III,
pp. 106f.
47. 'Mechanische stijheid en starheid';   '*geen* identieke repetitie';
'door het organische proces der Openbaring te gelijk geëischt en
beheerscht'; *ibid.*, p. 107.

oriented), his duality of essence and form, and his assumptions about form as a kind of prison for content. Yet, the need for flexibility is well-taken, and the warning against the tendency to level down the diversity of Scripture, historical and otherwise, hits target indeed. As methodical measures to ward off such a danger, we venture to propose the careful distinction of stages in biblical research. Let progress be step by step, with an eye for the specific contribution of each epoch, of each writer, and for the nuances in the use of words, viewpoints and conceptual schemes.   Interchange with critical scholarship, which ordinarily overrates differences and evolutions, will also serve as a protection.

D.A. Carson comes out with a precise suggestion.   'The *analogia fidei* should be used cautiously as an outer limit and as a final consideration rather than as the determining device.'[48] We would hesitate to restrict application of the analogy of faith to the *end* of the process of study; it also yields precious benefits in shaping our expectations, in stimulating our scientific imagination, in balancing our horizons. (Epistemology has grown more and more sensitive to the complexity of the factors at play in scientific work.) Yet, in practice, Carson's advice does show the same safer path we also try to beacon (and to follow).

Most thrilling and rewarding, especially for a systematic theologian, is the search for, and appeal to, a central truth or doctrine or structure. Yet, this aspect of the application of the *analogia fidei* is also fraught with the most serious risks. The slightest deviation of the compass needle, and the interpreter may land in a far country! The very love of the central theme, since our apprehension of it can never claim to be perfect, may hinder further progress, and block correction by Scripture. How could we escape unwitting arbitrariness and deformation? Our help comes from the general control of scriptural teachings, if we care diligently to enquire about it, and, especially, from

---

48. 'Unity and Diversity ...', p. 92.

hermeneutical lessons and hints offered by the biblical books themselves: 'meta-language' in Scripture and preliminary syntheses taught by divine inspiration provide us with invaluable aid. The New Testament writers' use and handling of the Old Testament, if we know how properly to assess it, is part of their authoritative teaching, and best educates our exegetical mind.[49] The *sedes doctrinae* should be the starting-points and basic guides for the study of corresponding topics: Galatians 4 and the Epistle to the Hebrews, for instance, on the relationship between Testaments.

Resorting to the analogy of faith, in the ways thus outlined, does not guarantee invulnerable rightness! Abuses and misuses threaten us still. But it will be the concrete expression of our stance as disciples: at the Master's feet, obeying and trusting his Word, trusting his Word regarding his Word. It will echo our confession: We have one Teacher ... (Mt.23:10).

---

49. The trustworthiness of their inspired teaching involves: (a) the validity of their judgement if they ascribe a definite meaning to an Old Testament passage, and (b), the validity of any reason they adduce in support of their claim. In many baffling cases, closer analysis has shown us that a modern believer *can* discern and appreciate this twofold validity, and find useful hermeneutical models under unfamiliar forms. We have strong reservations, therefore, about some of the theses of Richard N. Longenecker, 'Can We Reproduce the Exegesis of the New Testament?', *Tyndale Bulletin* 21, 1970, pp.3-38.

USING SCRIPTURE FOR THEOLOGY:
UNITY AND DIVERSITY IN OLD TESTAMENT THEOLOGY

The Old Testament as a Hermeneutical Problem

J. G. McCONVILLE

A special aspect of the question whether it is possible to do Christian theology is the question whether it is possible to do Old Testament theology. Indeed, there is a sense in which the possibility of the former depends upon the possibility of the latter. This is because the task of interpreting the Old Testament as such has been considered a distinctive part of the church's theological endeavour throughout its history, and indeed is arguably its central, most difficult hermeneutical task. Broadly speaking, the church's attitude to the Old Testament has been one of determination to keep it (*malgré* Marcion), 'from a sense that the roots of the Christian gospel are there, without having established, with any degree of unanimity, quite *how* it continues to address the church as the Word of God. The 'problem' of the Old Testament is caught in its very name - the 'Old' Testament, as distinct from the 'New' - and in the implication in the contrast that, because of the 'new' event witnessed to in Matthew-Revelation there is something *passé* about Genesis-Malachi (Chronicles).

Now, Marcion's was not the only kind of threat to the voice of the Old Testament in the church. If we may risk a generalization, the medieval church coped with the Old Testament by supposing that it did not teach anything which the church *could* not teach (*'scriptura non asserit nisi fidem catholicam'* - Augustine), and produced the powerful axis of *magisterium* and allegorical method.[1] The Reformation articulated new principles, which could be a basis for a genuine hearing of the Old Testament. Only a brave man would claim,

---

1.   A. H. J. Gunneweg, *Understanding the Old Testament,* London, 1978, pp. 40-42.

however, that the Reformation 'solved' the problem for good and all. For one thing, there continued to be 'rejections' of the Old Testament (notably in the nineteenth-century belief that it was essentially the literature of an alien and sub-Christian religion).[2] More fundamentally, however, the Reformation did not constitute a single or agreed solution. The approach of Luther is significantly different from that of Calvin, and I would suggest that in their different approaches we see the origins of the debate over the Old Testament as it is still carried on today. Let me say word or two about each.

Calvin (again at the risk of generalizing) tends to unify. That is to say, the Old Testament - and the Bible - is understood in terms of the over-arching concept of covenant. A coherent saving activity of God is revealed by the unified witness to it in the Scriptures of the Old and New Testaments. Thus the Scriptures as a whole have an equal standing and dignity. Now, it will immediately be seen that any approach in terms of system, or an overarching concept, may be open to the same kind of criticism as the medieval *magisterium*. [3]   That is to say, although a return to the 'plain sense' of Scripture opens it up in principle to be heard in all its richness and diversity, it may be in practice that it will only ever be heard in terms of covenantal theology. (And, indeed, the Reformation did not put an end to allegorizing interpretation either.)

Luther's approach to the Old Testament, as is well known, is based on his criterion that Scripture is only edifying inasmuch as it glorifies Christ. This hardly seems antithetical to Calvin's interests, but it does have the effect of bestowing unequal degrees of authority upon different biblical books, and Luther's views about Esther (a piece of Jewish propaganda) together with James (which seemed to contradict the doctrine of justification by faith) are familiar.   These are not mere

---

2.   *Ibid.* pp. 142 ff.
3.   Cf. D. Nineham, *Use and Abuse of the Bible*, London, 1976, pp. 45-59.

exceptions. Luther's whole hermeneutical method depends upon discerning polarities. The best-known is that of law and gospel. This is more subtle than a simple opposition of the Old Testament to the New, since law and gospel stand in (dialectical) tension with each other within each Testament, though law is more to the fore in the Old Testament.[4] The effect of this method, rather than a mere devaluing of the Old Testament, is to initiate an eclecticism in the study of biblical texts, of which Luther's attitude to Esther and James is an example. If Calvin's unifying approach to the Bible can result in our not hearing certain voices in the Old Testament, so too can Luther's polarizing approach. In this clash of opinions between the Reformation's two greatest theologians we have the seeds of the modern problem. That is, do we begin our reading of the Old Testament on the basis of a 'given' scheme? Or do we look at it first of all in its manifold character? I do not suggest that Luther and Calvin are the direct fathers of these two opposing modern approaches. Indeed, when modern scholars begin from diversity the claim usually is that their concern is to hear *all* that the Old Testament has to say, without the strict criterion of theological worth that Luther had, and clearly there have been many other influences upon modern scholarship in the intervening period.[5] Nevertheless, both Luther and Calvin are certainly (among the) ancestors of modern approaches, and we shall have cause to notice this influence from time to time. Their case is also instructive because it illustrates that a basic problem of method does exist, and requires a solution.

Modern Unifying Approaches

The *doyen* of those who, in modern times, have interpreted the Old Testament on the basis of a given scheme is W. Eichrodt,[6] who saw 'covenant' as a controlling concept. The striking resemblance to Calvin here (which is not as thoroughgoing as

---

4.   Gunneweg, *op. cit.*, pp. 51f.
5.   Gunneweg traces the interpretation of the Old Testament from the Reformation to modern times, *ibid.*, pp. 43-95.
6.   *Theology of the Old Testament*, 2 vols., London, 1961, 1967.

may appear at first[7]) does not mean that modern scholars have found any simple or obvious way of following the great Reformer into a unitary view of the Old Testament. On the contrary, the sad story of the search for a 'centre' in Old Testament theology suggests, by the very profusion of alleged 'centres', that the goal is elusive.[8] The objection to covenant in particular is that it does not deal with all the material in the Old Testament (*e.g.* Proverbs; Song; the non-historical material).[9] Most modern writers, in pronouncing the search hopeless, say that the idea of a centre can be maintained only in terms of concepts which are so bland as to be not very helpful (*e.g.* Hasel, having ruled out all other possibilities, opts simply for 'God'[10]). However, considerations like this have not prevented some scholars, even in the wake of criticism of Eichrodt, from writing theologies which are essentially systematic. Examples are W. Zimmerli[11] and, among evangelical scholars, W. Dyrness and W. J. Dumbrell.[12] These, indeed, are satisfactory in different degrees,[13] and Dumbrell's, which is an excellent apology for 'covenant' as the controlling concept, does not actually claim that his work

7. As has been observed by J. E. Goldingay, *Diversity and Unity in Old Testament Theology, Vetus Testamentum* 34 (1984), p. 155, there is full acknowledgement of the diversity of Old Testament statements in Eichrodt. That may render his insistence on imposing a scheme the more striking.
8. Cf. G. Hasel, *Old Testament Theology: Basic Issues in the Current Debate*, Grand Rapids, 1972, pp 78ff.; H. Graf Reventlow, *Problems of Old Testament Theology in the Twentieth Century*, London, 1985, pp. 125ff., for accounts of the search for a centre.
9. Hasel, p. 79.
10. *Ibid.*, pp. 99-103; and *cf.* Gunneweg's criticism, *op. cit.*, p 140.
11. W. Zimmerli, *Old Testament Theology in Outline*, Edinburgh, 1978, and see J. E. Goldingay, *Approaches to Old Testament Interpretation*, Leicester,1981, p. 28-9.
12. W. J. Dumbrell, *Covenant and Creation*, Exeter, 1984. W. Dyrness,*Themes in Old Testament Theology*, Exeter,1979.
13. Dyrness's hardly does justice to the forward flow and ever-changing face of the Old Testament.

constitutes an Old Testament theology as such. Nevertheless, the sense that the Old Testament is characterized by unity and has an organizing concept or concepts may not be finally contradicted by the lack of unanimity over the latter. And indeed it is highly questionable whether an irreducible 'centre' - namely 'God' - is as 'bland' as is alleged. Even Gunneweg, who is eloquent in his hostility to 'centres', comes back to a position which is not so very different, in the end, from Hasel's, for he justifies the Old Testament ultimately because it makes a basically similar assessment of *God and Man* to that of the New Testament. God is transcendent, yet meets man.[14] I believe that an adequate hermeneutic of the Old Testament must resort to concepts which control and unify. I hope this will emerge further as we look now at approaches which begin from the belief that the Old Testament is fundamentally characterized by diversity.

Approaches Beginning from Diversity

It needs no demonstration that diversity of some kind exists in the Old Testament. There are differences at the level of type of literature. The Old Testament contains texts which are poetic, prophetic, liturgical, narrative, legal, theological/speculative. These can overlap. But the point is that the Old Testament makes an immediate impression of variety, as opposed to system, in its statements about God. (Hence Barr's and Nineham's insistence that the Old Testament is simply not directly translatable into systematic theology.) This impression may be strengthened when we remember that the Old Testament came into being over a long period (much longer than that in which the New Testament developed), and in the context of a history which saw vast changes in the character of Israel (slaves in Egypt - loosely associated tribes in Canaan - monarchy/ies - exiles - weak imperial satrapy). This essential disparateness of the Old Testament was an important factor for G. von Rad in his Old Testament theology, often cited as the antithesis to

---

14. *Op. cit.,* pp. 225f.

Eichrodt's. For him the Old Testament is the deposit of Israel's multi-faceted experience of God. His method is to describe the various and successive 'theologies' of the Old Testament, without any pretence that they amount to a unified witness. Now the implication of von Rad's approach is that the diversity in the Old Testament is more profound than differences of genre, date, *etc.* There are, for him, distinct theological currents within the Old Testament, which may resemble each other in certain respects, but strongly differ from each other in others. *E.g.,* different theological systems are represented by the Priestly and Deuteronomistic writings. Eichrodt, of course, would not dissent from this. The difference is that von Rad has made such differences the key to his method. The strength of von Rad is that he very much captures the forward flow of the Old Testament, rescuing it from a static, over-systematic approach. He seriously attempts to let *all* of the Old Testament speak. (For this reason his is often more text-based and just plain useful than Eichrodt.) The great weakness becomes manifest when we attempt to turn his observations of what Israel believed into something that the Church can confess. The most obvious reason for this is that the method fundamentally postulates important theological differences. What then should we believe? The situation is not improved when we bear in mind that, for von Rad, Israel's experience of God does not necessarily correspond to the history of Israel as it is reconstructed by the modern historian. Von Rad leaves us, therefore, even apart from the considerations of multiple theologies, without a way of believing what Israel believed that does any justice to a meaningful relationship between faith and knowledge. The inevitable suggestion of von Rad's work (though I think he intended the opposite) is that it is exceedingly hazardous to base any faith-position on the witness of the Old Testament.

Von Rad has probably set the tone in modern scholarly discussion. John Goldingay says of certain contemporary writers on the Old Testament that for them 'diversity is the starting-point, and unity or coherence or inter-relationship is a much more problematical question, if it arises at all'.[15] Goldingay himself, however, is concerned to 'acknowledge diversity, without canonizing arbitrariness'.[16] He does this by postulating 'trajectories' in biblical thinking about certain themes, that is, a range of opinions within the Old Testament on a given subject, encompassing opposing extremes and a point of equilibrium.[17] Thus, on the relationship between the activity of God and that of man, he sees apocalyptic at one end of the spectrum (emphasizing God's acts), Esther at the other (emphasizing human initiative), and Isaiah avoiding both extremes, recognizing both the call and will of God while functioning as a statesman beside the king. On this topic of faith Isaiah has the 'fullest insight' within an inner-biblical dialectic.[18] Goldingay goes further and appears to see polarity as belonging to the essential character of the Bible. In this he appeals to Ebeling's observations, taking his cue from Luther, of how polarity functions in biblical interpretations, Scripture indeed having essentially a polar structure which reflects 'its comprehensive relation to life'. The basic polar relationship identified by Ebeling is that of God and Israel, other associated tensions being election and universalism, Israel as a political entity and as a religious community, cultic piety and prophetic piety, individual and community, openness and distinctiveness, scepticism and confidence, judgement and grace, law and promise. Goldingay adds creation and redemption, exodus and exile, word and event.[19]

---

15. J. E.Goldingay, *art. cit.*, p. 157.
16. *Ibid.*, p 160.
17. He thus follows J. M. Robinson and H. Koester, *Trajectories through Early Christianity*, Philadelphia, 1971.
18. *Ibid.*, pp. 160-163, also citing P. D. Hanson, *The Dawn of Apocalyptic*, Philadelphia, 1975.
19. *Ibid.*, pp. 166f., G. Ebeling, *Luther*, London, 1970, p. 25; *ZThK* 77 (1980), pp. 276f., *The Study of Theology*, London, 1979, pp. 19f.

J. G. McConville

Kinds of Diversity

The approach adopted by Goldingay we have seen to owe
something to Ebeling, and perhaps in turn to Luther. It is
difficult to avoid the conclusion that, as with Luther, different
parts of Scripture, on this view, speak with varying degrees of
theological acumen (and therefore authority?).

Do we, then, have diversity in the Old Testament?   The
question can only be met by another question, namely, what is
meant by diversity? Goldingay seems to speak about different
kinds of diversity without alerting us to the fact that he is doing
so.   That is, he speaks on the one hand about the simple
disagreement between biblical authors over given issues, and on
the other he leans on a rather sophisticated idea according to
which polarity is somehow a necessary feature of biblical
language about God. We must, therefore, set the discussion on
a sounder basis, and can do so, I suggest, by identifying two
kinds of diversity which exist in the Old Testament.

First, there is a class of polarity which is inherent in the
theology of the Old Testament.   The undergirding one in this
category is that of God and Israel (mankind), but along with this
come such others as law and grace, God known and unknown,
ritual (cultic) and spontaneous (prophetic) religion. All of these
have been treated by at least some Old Testament scholars in
terms of conflict and polemic.   Modern treatments of
Deuteronomy illustrate the point.   It is common today for
Deuteronomy to be seen as a succession of literary 'layers',
each characterized by its own theological attitude in terms of the
relationship between law and grace. Thus von Rad discerned
in Deuteronomy 'a declension from grace into law',[20] meaning
that the earliest form of the book had essentially a theology of
grace, while later expansions were increasingly legalistic.

20. G. von Rad, 'Promised Land and Yahweh's Land', in *The Problem
of the Hexateuch and Other Essays*, Edinburgh & London, 1966,
p. 91.

Some detailed treatments of Deuteronomy have attempted to work this out more or less verse by verse.[21]   The thinking may be illustrated by Deut. 7:11,12, each verse expressing the need for obedience to God, the former, however, motivating it in terms of gratitude for God's love and faithfulness (as in vv.6-10), while the latter seems to make obedience the prerequisite of God's covenant-keeping.   For scholars such as L. Perlitt, this is a jarring juxtaposition which is only explicable by appeal to secondary, legalistic expansion.[22]   Now the whole approach is open to the criticism that it has failed to comprehend the character of the rhetoric of Deuteronomy.   Others have shown more acuteness here, and recognized that such juxtapositions belong precisely to the heart of Deuteronomy's message, and indeed that such tensions are frequently held together in Deuteronomy by means of complex literary structures such as extended chiasmus.[23]   In other words the rhetoric of Deuteronomy profoundly matches the complexity of its theology.   Law-keeping is not only response to God's grace, but it also oils the wheels of the continuing relationship between God and Israel.   Deuteronomy thus deals in its own way with an antinomy inherent (I think) in all religion, and which the New Testament takes up at various points too (Romans 6; James).   The tension between law and grace, then, is not to be seen in terms of conflict, confrontation, polemic (the way of Hegel) but rather as that which belongs to theology, and which the Old Testament can present as such.   If one 'pole' is

---

21. The most recent standard commentary on Deuteronomy is A. D. H. Mayes (New Century Bible), in which this kind of concept is fundamental.

22. L. Perlitt, *Bundestheologie in Alten Testament*, Neukirchen-Vluyn, 1969, p. 61.

23. N. Lohfink, *Das Hauptgebot: eine Untersuchung Literarischer Einleitungsfragen Zu Dt. 5-11*, Rome, 1963, p. 240, insists on the integrity of 7:12 in its context.

24. See Eichrodt, *op. cit.*, Vol.1, pp. 286-8, for his synthesis – in antinomy - of those characteristics of God which make him distant (holiness, wrath) and those which bring him near (righteousness, love).

sometimes more in view than the other, that too is in the nature of the case, since imbalance must be corrected by counter-balance (as a high-wire walker who leans too far one way will compensate by dipping his balancing-pole the other). Thus it is that in certain situations there can be an emphasis on the preaching of law (*e.g.* Amos) while in others there is an emphasis on grace (Isaiah 40-66). Even here, however, the one-sidedness of the preaching can be overemphasised. There is no prophetic book which lacks the element of grace and promise. The widespread denial of Amos 9:11-15 to the prophet Amos is arguably only tenable in terms of a theory of divergent theologies.

I have used law and grace as an example of the kind of polarity which is inherent in Old Testament theology. The other polarities which were named in this category (God's knowability yet unknowability,[24] ritual and spontaneous religion[25]) could have been treated similarly. We might also mention here the poles of individual and community,[26] and even faith and doubt/scepticism. This latter is sometimes treated as a deep divide within Old Testament religion, the way of scepticism even being seen as an 'alternative to Yahwism' by one writer.[27] Seeds of scepticism are seen, for example, in a Psalm such as 73, contrasted with the more serene confidence

---

25. It has often been held that the Old Testament 'outgrows' ritual religion and thus initiates a trend which continues and is completed in the New Testament. Passages in the prophets (*e.g.* Isaiah 1:11-17; Jeremiah 7:1-5,21-23; Micah 6:6-8) and in the Psalms (Pss. 40; 50) are cited as evidence. However, moderating voices are also to be heard, *e.g.* J. Bright, *Jeremiah*, New York, 1965, pp. 56f. See also my 'The Place of Ritual in Old Testament Religion', *IBS* 35 (1981), pp. 120-33, for an argument for the complementarity of ritual and non-ritual dimensions of worship in the Old Testament (and beyond).

26. For a critique of the old idea of corporate personality see J. W. Rogerson, *Anthropology and the Old Testament*, Oxford, 1978.

27. J. L. Crenshaw, *Old Testament Wisdom: an Introduction*, London, 1981, p. 208.

of Ps. 37. It can be seen indeed as a topic of the lament Psalms in general (Why hast thou cast us off, O Lord?), but comes to a head in Ecclesiastes. Here too, however, faith and doubt should be seen as so closely related as to be implied by each other. This indeed is always the context in which doubts are expressed in the Old Testament, and they function - whether explicitly or implicitly - to put faith on a sounder basis.[28]

So much then for diversity that is in the nature of the case. The second broad category is that which arises from the fact that the Old Testament tells a story of God's dealings with man (Israel) which develops and moves through many phases. There are many examples: i. *Creation and Redemption.* The dialectic here is precipitated by historical events, namely disobedience, with one archetypal act of disobedience at the fountainhead. Redemption, therefore, is always restoration of the former played out in history. ii. *Politics and Religion.* This too is a product of God's historical dealing with mankind, this time in election, because in the course of his redeeming work he calls out a *nation* within which to teach religious devotion. Both politics and religion are necessities (not necessarily antithetical, as Isaiah shows) which co-exist as long as the nation does. The prophetic critique of the political leadership in its actual corruption never implies the impossibility of religion being cultivated within such structures, not that the religious community cannot also be political. (Of course the community, by way of an historical contingency, does become more religious and less political at a point in time.) iii. *Election and Universalism.* These come into severe conflict in Deuteronomy and Joshua, where the nation which is elected in order that the nations in general might be blessed by it (Gen.12:3) is mandated to destroy nations in order to occupy their land. Election can thus appear to be self-serving in Deuteronomy, and no doubt later exclusivistic nationalism appealed (and appeals) to this. I

---

28. Goldingay, *art.cit.,* is not far from this position, and indeed his analysis of the faith-doubt relationship (based on W. Brueggemann, 'Psalms and the Life of Faith', *JSOT* 12 (1980) pp. 5-16, 24-30) is illuminating.

have argued elsewhere that the paradox of election for the nations' salvation is worked out in history in conjunction with the theological topic of due punishment for sin, and in a context in which 'nationalism' (of which 'Israel' is necessarily a manifestation) is part of a less-than-ideal, fallen world and consequently fragmented humanity.[29]   Other opposites such as judgement and mercy, exodus and exile only become problematic if each pole is raised to an absolute (as 'exodus' has been in Liberation Theology), rather than being seen against a shifting historical background.   (The corporate-individual tension thus has an historical dimension too, the 'individualism' of Ezek. 18 being rather an insistence in the context of exile - the apparently final cataclysm - that each generation remains morally responsible before God.)

Unity, Diversity & Exegesis

In the foregoing I have been suggesting that where diversity exists in the Old Testament it does not always have the kind of significance which some writers attribute to it.   We have observed particular diversities, and found that they could be explained either by the complexity of the business of depicting the relationship between God and man or by the historical vicissitudes through which Israel passed.   The question still remaining is whether there is a kind of diversity in the Old Testament whose *essence* is discord or conflict?   Are there competing beliefs, ideologies, attitudes among which we, as those who seek to confess a biblical faith, are compelled to select some and reject others?   A complete answer to this could only be provided by an exegesis of the entire Old Testament (which we can hardly attempt here! - though Keil and Delitzsch attempted it over 100 years ago).   We can say, however, that the answer lies in the direction of exegesis.

Of course it is not just as simple as that, since there is no *agreed* exegesis of the Old Testament.   Sharp disagreements on

---

29.   In *Evangel* 13:1 (1985), pp. 2-5.

particular points can occur even among those who are broadly in sympathy, more profound disagreements among those who are not. And this idea of 'sympathy' points us to the fact that exegesis is for no-one an independent exercise, objectively extracting *the* meaning of a given text. This is so because all interpreters work with a concept of what it is that they are doing, which in turn involves belief of some sort about the Bible. And even where that 'belief' is 'believing', agreement remains outstanding because of divergent opinions as to what biblical authority means in practice. The point has nothing to do with obscurantism. Indeed, exegesis and theology, hermeneutics and biblical authority go inextricably together. These dualities are not in conflict. The best understanding of 'systematic theology' is not the static rationalism caricatured by scholars such as D. E. Nineham,[30] but articulation of the counsel of God in still-learning submission to all that the Scriptures have to say.[31] True biblical interpretation is a dialectic between understanding of the letter (the jot and tittle) and understanding of the whole. Now with this idea of the 'whole', I have re-entered a debate which I touched on earlier, namely the question of canonicity. Is the extent of the canon 'up for grabs' (in the manner of Luther) or is it an immutable datum of hermeneutics (in the manner of Calvin)?[32] The former view is always likely to result in some sort of 'canon' within a 'canon', since 'inconvenient' books/passages/texts can be dismissed or at least devalued. The availablility of this recourse can mean that exegesis is not pushed to its limits, answers are too quickly arrived at, conflicts too readily postulated. The idea of 'dialectic' in Scripture can become so powerful that texts in general are viewed as being the result of conflict or polemic

---

30. *Op. cit.*
31. As championed by J. I. Packer.
32. Obviously the question is raised whether any one of the ancient 'canons' can be taken to be the 'true' one. Current critical orthodoxy tends to hold that the canon was in a fluid state at the birth of Christianity. However, see now R. T. Beckwith, *The Old Testament Canon of the New Testament Church,* London, 1985 (And Protestantism) was well established by the turn of the eras.

between competing views (one, or some, of which, therefore, must be rejected). An example is Deut.18:1-8, often seen as the deposit of a long struggle between rival groups for recognition as the legitimate priesthood, a postulate which close examination reveals to be totally unnecessary.[33] In my view, then, this (Lutheran) view of canon leads to a kind of exegesis which makes insufficient demands of itself. Only a rigorous view of the authoritativeness of the whole canon of Scripture (understood to be represented, as regards the Old Testament, in the Hebrew Bible) releases the interpreter from the danger of subjectivity, and requires that any text be understandable in terms of all of Scripture, even if that means modifying slightly what one believes 'Scripture says'. A canon which can in principle be abbreviated, on the other hand, leads to the postulation of 'diversities' which are in fact illusory.

We return, in the light of these remarks, to Goldingay's 'trajectories'. In his discussion of the idea of human self-help in relation to the need for God's intervention he regarded the prophet Isaiah as most satisfactorily expressing the need to affirm both poles of the paradox, while Esther and Daniel (apocalyptic) leaned too far in one direction or the other. It is not clear from his treatment to what extent, or whether at all, Esther and Daniel may be read with profit (at least in connection with this theme). Yet there is in some sense a devaluation of these two books, which implies a certain view of canon. However, if Esther and Daniel are approached on the opposite assumption that they have some vital, distinctive role to play within Scripture, very different conclusions are likely to be reached. In fact the (very fashionable) view of Esther as a tract advocating self-help rather than reliance on God simply misses much that Esther has to say. It seems to me that Esther proclaims no 'other gospel' on the question of where to place one's trust. On the contrary, the book represents a firm belief

33. For an exegesis based on an assumption of polemic see Gunneweg, *Leviten und Priester,* Göttingen, 1965. Against this see the present writer's *Law & Theology in Deuteronomy,* Sheffield, 1984, pp. 124-153.

that proper human action fuses mysteriously with something lying directly behind events, which is well beyond human power to control. Why not say explicitly, then, that this power is God? This question is not answered by a rejection of the 'God-hypothesis', but rather initiates the search for other hermeneutical clues. My own view of the matter is that the absence of God's name in the book is, paradoxically, a kind of theodicy, a recognition that God often seems absent in the daily life of the believer, yet in reality is very present.[34] Here, then, we have something that Isaiah does not have, a message perhaps particularly pressing in certain situations, while Isaiah's (with his counsel against reliance on human institutions instead of God) is pressing in others.

Here I want to notice a paradox. The approach to the Old Testament which stresses diversity (wherever, that is, it retains an interest in hearing and using Scripture confessionally) can end in a flattening and a uniformity (as we have seen the Isaiah-Esther-Daniel spectrum reduced to the lowest common denominator of Isaiah). In contrast, where the unity of the Old Testament is regarded as the primary hermeneutical datum, the real diversity of the material can emerge, to the richer benefit of the believing community. This is important, for the unity I am advocating is not a ground for pan-harmonization. Nor should it be thought that harmonization at all costs is the way to do justice to the Old Testament's unity. The unity I am concerned for is one which is in contrast to the idea of competing theologies or ideologies. I would be less interested in pursuing a large-scale harmonization of Kings and Chronicles, for it seems to me that the significance of the presence of these two large books is as much explained by their differences as their similarities. The same could be said of the laws of Deuteronomy in comparison with those of Exodus-Numbers. In such cases the meaning of books emerges from the different ways in which they organize and present basically similar

---

34.   I have developed this in 'Diversity and Obscurity in Old Testament Books', *Anvil* 3 (1986), pp. 33-47.

materials.[35]   Thus Deuteronomy in its laws about cult emphasizes such things as the brotherhood of the people, God's readiness to bless, the need for obedience, in general terms, to God's commandments; while laws on similar subjects in Exodus-Numbers relate more directly to holiness, understood ritually, and ritual instructions in general.   These are obviously not mutually exclusive.

An Approach to Old Testament Theology

It is clear from all that has been said that the Old Testament is marked by both unity and diversity.   I have argued that all the . difference in the world is made to exegesis depending on whether the interpreter begins with a concept of unity or a postulate of diversity.   Having argued for the former approach, on the basis of a view of canon, I have maintained that, nevertheless, exegesis must do justice to the individuality of texts.   I want finally to indicate three elements which I think must be present in any adequate Old Testament theology.

1.   *A recognition of the forward movement, or historical character, of the Old Testament revelation.*   We say that this factor in the Old Testament accounted for certain kinds of diversity which are found there.   The 'historicality' of the Old Testament is, for von Rad, its primary characteristic and determines the way in which its theology should be written. Von Rad has seen something important.   Because the Old Testament has so much material spread over so long a period there is a sense in which it can *only* be described chronologically.   (Thus Old Testament theologies which are rigidly 'systematic' are under a great disadvantage.)   Eichrodt actually does this also, except that he does it section by section in dogmatic categories.   More important than this pragmatic

---

35.   See my *Law and Theology in Deuteronomy*, pp. 90f.   *Cf.* p. 87 for an example of how one of Deuteronomy's laws (that of tithe) should be interpreted in context.

consideration, however, is the fact that the Old Testament does point forward to and find its fulfilment in Christ.

2. *A theological-unifying element.* This is what, on the face of it, Eichrodt has and von Rad has not, though Eichrodt is in fact just as ready to accommodate kinds of diversity which I have called illusory. Eichrodt, does, however, point in the direction of making statements about God (in the sense of systematic theology) on the basis of the Old Testament. This is, as surely as von Rad's, a correct instinct, for those at least who see the Old Testament as a basis (with the New Testament) for confession. It is possible to do this by looking for what the various biblical books have in common, explicitly or implicitly, in their view of God and man. When one begins from an assumption of unity, naturally, this common body of Old Testament 'opinion' will be the greater. (Again, however, I stress that the individuality of books must be respected.)

To say this, however, is not quite the same as saying that there must be a 'centre' of Old Testament theology. It may be, indeed, that to identify 'God' as the centre of the Old Testament is not as bland as some have suggested. It is probably better to postulate some complex of ideas or 'centres' as a way of doing more justice to the whole Old Testament. Yet perhaps the search for a centre has proved unsatisfying because the Old Testament is not ultimately a thing in itself but rather a part of the whole Bible, whose 'centre' is Christ. This is not to argue for a Christological exegesis of the Old Testament which pays little heed to the demands of an historical methodology (in the manner of Vischer). Rather it is to say that it is impossible to appropriate the Old Testament for Christian theology without recognizing its 'preparatory' character, and its complementarity with the New Testament in the life of the Church.

3. *An existential element* . I include this, finally, as a kind of corrective to the former two. It is meant to recognize the fact that the Old Testament is the deposit of people's actual experience of God in many situations over many centuries.

There was in that experience a 'nowness', albeit infinitely repeated and taking ever new forms, which did not necessarily see itself in terms of a grandiose 'forward movement'. The heritage of Israel's knowledge of God, in great expanses of time, flowed into daily living that was mundane, and provided a self-understanding and grounds for worship. Countless men and women were, in their own experience, the recipients of God's salvation, without any conscious reference to the fact that they were within some grand scheme (though their theologians may have had such a consciousness), or that *their* experience was only in some way preparatory, inferior to what was prepared for generations to come.[36] This is an element which theologies have often failed to accommodate. Von Rad could find no place for the Wisdom literature in his history-oriented scheme; and 'centre'-based theologies can struggle equally to do it justice. (It is not only in Wisdom that we glimpse the routine of Israel's life; *cf.* the Psalms.) The complete Old Testament theology will allow for the Old Testament as experience of God. That is to say, it will recognize that the Old Testament has an element that is neither strictly forward-moving, nor constitutive of 'theology', but creative of religious experience, worship and life-style, and continues to function in this way for the believer and believing community. (Song of Songs, Psalms and the Wisdom books may be specially mentioned in this connection, though the narrative books can function similarly.) Once again we can, of course, transpose this into a higher key, for in Christ Christians have the experience of salvation. (Note the 'wisdom' language, incidentally, of Colossians 2:3 - the riches of wisdom/knowledge in Christ.)

Christian experience of God and salvation is, therefore, qualitatively different from that of the Old Testament saint. The latter's, however, was equally real, and the Christological fulfilment does not abolish the 'usefulness' of the Old

---

36. Gunneweg has rightly insisted, on this point, *Understanding the Old. Testament,* pp. 230f.

Testament in this respect. Indeed, biblical ethics must always lean heavily on the Old Testament. It seems to me that a knowledge of what God-likeness is cannot be read off the pages of the Gospels without some dialectic taking place between what we see in Christ there and what the Old Testament teaches and suggests about character. Vriezen's view that Calvin's unifying approach to the Old Testament inevitably issues in an allegorical interpretation of the Song of Songs is misguided.[37] The two Testaments as a resource for the building of Christian character must be read both in their own terms and as they reflect upon each other.

All three of these elements could obviously be developed much further (into an Old Testament theology!). I have tried to indicate some of the problems, real and imaginary, which confront the Old Testament interpreter, and to outline ways in which they may be overcome in a manner which does justice to the unity of the revelation of God.

---

37. T. C. Vriezen, *An Outline of Old Testament Theology*, Oxford, 1962, p. 8.

UNITY AND DIVERSITY IN CHRISTIAN THEOLOGY

GERALD BRAY

The theme is fundamental to our common concern. The vastness of the subject and the limited extent of the time available make it especially important to say, at the beginning, what this paper is - and just as important, what it is not! It is an examination of the basic issues which confront theologians of every tendency and tradition when they attempt to write some kind of systematic theology. Now that traditional denominational labels have lost much of their earlier importance it has become necessary for theologians, even those writing from a particular confessional standpoint, to give adequate consideration to other viewpoints and methods. In this respect, the ecumenical movement has become a practical reality for all of us, and so too has the need to understand more clearly the lines of convergence and divergence which bind us to, and separate us from, other theological endeavours. On the other hand, this paper is not a model theological system, and for that reason, a good many things have been left out. In particular, relatively little will be said about the ecclesiological differences which so obviously separate Christians from one another. This is not because I think such differences do not matter, but because from the purely theological standpoint, they are often of secondary importance. In many cases, they are also far too complex, requiring treatment too detailed to fit readily into the dimensions of a paper such as this one.

The first imperative for any discussion of this subject is the need to define what the current situation is. Next we shall look at the relationship between what is and what ought to be, allowing of course for the presupposition and outlook which are bound to govern one's assessment of this ideal. Thirdly, we shall have to consider the limits of what is tolerable within the Christian church as a whole and what is simply un-Christian. Fourthly, we shall look at what might be tolerable within a given sub-

system of Christian theology but need not be accepted by all
Christians – indeed, may not be acceptable to them, assuming
that they have developed another sub-system in which a
particular formulation is uncongenial. It will be obvious from
the start that in many ways it is this fourth area which raises the
greater possibilities for dissent, since one of the major issues of
our time is whether a particular sub-system can claim universal
(and probably also exclusive) validity, or whether it is necessary
to accept that current Christian theology is fundamentally a
grouping of sub-systems which can possibly be transcended but
which can never be merged into a single whole.

Synchronic and Diachronic

Turning then, first of all, to the current situation, we have to say
that systematic theology today has to respond to two competing,
though not always equally powerful, pressures, which can be
called respectively the synchronic and the diachronic (or in
simpler language, the contemporary and the historical). Of the
two, the diachronic is obviously the more rooted, the more
institutional.   The churches, denominations and spiritual
movements to which theologians today belong are all the
products of historical development. Often they bear witness to
this in confessional documents which enshrine one particular
tradition, or perhaps a compromise between particular
traditions, and the contemporary systematic theologian is
obliged to acknowledge this fact, whether by commitment,
criticism or outright opposition to his own confessional
heritage.

The synchronic pressure is very different. Often more dynamic
and attractive than the diachronic, it moves in the direction of
relevance, simplicity and unity. It may not be ecumenical in
any formal sense, but it is certainly ecumenical in practice, a
tendency which is bound to work against the rigid
confessionalism of an earlier era.   The latter has not
disappeared, but under the impact of synchronic pressures, the
concept of confession has given way to tradition, that of

denomination to identity - influential and valuable things, but things which are seen primarily in a relative context of mutually co-existing sub-cultures which are or can be united by a deeper set of factors. This viewpoint, incidentally, is found among both liberals and conservatives in the modern church. Indeed, one might even say that the chief difference between the liberal and the conservative is that the liberal generally derives his basis of unity from synchronic elements, whilst the conservative generally derives it from diachronic ones. Liberal unity thus involves a common outlook on the world which may well owe much of its essence to non-Christian factors; conservative unity looks back to a time before the emergence of separate theological traditions and tends to be expressed more in the mutual confession of doctrines and adoption of practices common to the early church as a whole. In terms of historical theology, the liberal typically emphasizes the period since Schleiermacher; the conservative, the period before Chalcedon. Intervening eras - the Middle Ages, or the Reformation - remain the preserve of those conservatives who have not been seriously affected by the synchronic pressures of our time. Occasionally they may even be people who by education or temperament do not accept that there are today synchronic pressures widely different from the diachronic ones, and as a result they may continue to develop and proclaim a particular theological tradition as a viable option in contemporary society. But although such people can claim the weight of history on their side, they are now generally dismissed as reactionaries by the mainline churches and, among the younger generation at least, relegated to the sectarian fringe.

This, then, is the situation in the church today. But is it necessarily what should be? Apart from a small minority of *laissez-faire*, don't-rock-the-boat types, many of whom understandably go far up the ecclesiastical careers ladder, most thinking theologians would answer in the negative. The difficulty of course, is that the motives which prompt this negativeness are very different in each case. Some are impatient with the residual power of diachronic pressures and want to see them disappear as fast as possible. The charismatic and renewal movements act as a powerful solvent of tradition, because even though the content of their faith may in some respects appear to be arch-conservative, it is also almost entirely non-reflective, and therefore easily disregarded. A simple example of this is the well-known fact that charismatic or renewed Protestants are almost always happy, even eager, to co-operate in every way with Roman Catholics of a similar type, and that both are negative towards the more conventionally traditionalist members of their own denominations, in spite of their formal theological agreement with them.

On the other hand, there are those who seek a renewed confessionalism, a return to the diachronic pressures which continue to be felt in the churches. These people demand a stricter adherence to official confessions of faith, and may even seek to exclude others, not only from their fellowship but from the wider church. In normal times, these people are neither very numerous nor very articulate, but they come into their own when something extraordinary occurs - for example, when the Bishop of Durham appears to deny the virgin birth and resurrection of Christ. Then it becomes clear that they have a latent strength beyond their apparent numbers, and that the synchronic pressure groups are rather flabby or elitist by comparison.

A third group, to which theologically-minded conservative Evangelicals usually seem to belong, want to preserve some kind of balance between the synchronic and the diachronic. 'Balanced Christianity' has frequently been criticised for being more interested in balance than in Christianity, but it would perhaps be fairer to suggest that it is a poor solution to an admittedly difficult problem, because the synchronic and diachronic pressures which it seeks to match are different from each other in kind. They cannot be held together in balance because they are not mutually complementary. In practice every theologian responds more readily to one of them, and in the light of that response, formulates an attitude to the other derived not from it but from the approach to which he is already committed. In extreme cases, outlined above, this may mean almost total rejection of the other, but more often it becomes a selective acceptance of what the other has to offer. Thus a conservative traditionalist will be constrained to relate his views to those of the wider church, and to its needs today, whilst the liberal may have to acquiesce, more or less willingly, in the classical symbolism and liturgy which have always defined Christian and denominational identity. He may seek to alter them by judicial means, but usually he will be content to live with freedom of interpretation - much to the chagrin of conservatives!

In trying to decide which of these pressures should be allowed to form the basic framework for a systematic theology, it is necessary to look at their respective merits. The synchronic pressure is a very attractive one, because it affects us all, wherever we come from, it belongs to our time and therefore appears to be novel and original - qualities which are virtuous in our society - and because, after all, we cannot escape them for long if we want to live in our own time. The danger is that those who succumb to them are liable to display a kind of zeal without knowledge, enthusiasm unencumbered by the experience of history and probably not interested in it. The diachronic pressure, on the other hand, gives its adherents knowledge, though it may come with or without zeal. Although we must deplore the latter, we ought to recognise it as a perversion, a scandal - *corruptio optimi pessima* – not as inherent in the diachronic option. In spite of the attractions of the synchronic option, I believe that the historical character of revelation forces us to prefer the diachronic one, because only with knowledge are we equipped to judge and control the spiritual forces of our age.

This of course brings us to the third point. If the diachronic approach is preferable overall, how far can it bend to accommodate various synchronic pressures? I have already indicated that a total merger is impossible, but a total rejection of the one is impracticable since, like it or not, we are compelled to live in our own time and cannot return to the securities of an imaginary past. We are then left with the boundaries of permissible selection, which so far have never been properly defined. We can be fairly certain that traditional language, formulae and rites will be maintained. Generally speaking, the closer one gets to the man in the pew the more traditional theological expression will be. Recent experience has shown that radical change at the popular level is only possible when the man in the pew has little power - or when the pew is empty. Surveys in England have shown that non-churchgoers generally resent the recent changes in the liturgy and prefer traditional weddings and funerals. Certainly it will be a long time before 'thee' and 'thou' disappear from *Songs of Praise*. The BBC, unlike the church, knows all about audience ratings!

Of course, it is also true that the higher one's personal commitment becomes, the more likely one is to look for radical change, especially if the starting point of one's faith was well outside the bounds of the church and one's progress has remained impervious to theological instruction. But no theologian can be content to rest his case on popular piety alone, if only because a major part of his task is to inform that piety and give it deep and lasting roots in the Word of God. The theologian is left then with a somewhat ambiguous attitude towards practical change of a liturgical or stylistic nature, where individual taste is likely to be at least as influential as theological conviction. And this of course, is a problem. For to what extent is it possible to alter details of ritual and not change the theology thus represented? To appeal to the practice of the Reformers in this matter merely highlights the difficulty. They introduced radical changes, not because they liked change, but because they had a new theology which needed to express itself. In other words, the changes of the Reformation did not come mainly from synchronic pressures outside the church, but from diachronic pressures resulting from the rediscovery of a forgotten message. Where this rediscovery did not take place, synchronic pressures, which at the time of the Renaissance

63

operated in favour of an open Bible and a vernacular liturgy, were actually resisted with considerable success.

The modern susceptibility to synchronic pressures is therefore not a new Reformation but quite a different phenomenon. At the most serious level, it can be seen in the widespread surrender of modern theology to the secular philosopher of the age. It may be objected that Schleiermacher's adoption of Kant is really no different from Aquinas' adoption of Aristotle, or Augustine's predilection for Neoplatonism. But against this is the intriguing fact that St. Thomas' Aristotelianism and Augustine's Neoplatonism have been a problem only since the time of Schleiermacher. Before then, not even Luther or Calvin noticed the philosophical background of the classical theologians, whom they certainly did not despise as being corrupt. The theological degeneration of the post-apostolic, or even of the post-Easter church was a discovery of the nineteenth century which was only possible because that century was in revolt against the diachronic pressures which were then felt to be constricting theological development. For the first time, *Histories of Dogma* were written, giving a detailed outline of this process, and ending inevitably with the Reformation which was regarded as both the last phase of dogmatic development and the beginning of a new wave of freedom which after three centuries would liberate the church from dogma altogether.

The synchronic pressures of the time were made the basis of the theological agenda - evolution, progress, natural science and so on. When, as was inevitable, the church which was wedded to the spirit of the nineteenth century became widowed in the twentieth, a new and more flexible liberalism appeared. Synchronic pressures continued to dominate the theological agenda, but now they were conditioned by a new awareness of built-in obsolescence. Today the theologians of liberation, feminism, ecology and so on know they are not writing for eternity. Their sole aim is to achieve the academic equivalent of box-office success right now. John Robinson's *Honest to God*, for example, has been translated into as many languages and sold about as many copies as Calvin's *Institutes*, but whilst the former is already dated and going out of print, the latter continues to be read and printed much as it always has been.

Of course, modern theologians of Robinson's type select from the synchronic range of pressures available, and achieve notoriety by focusing on one or two particularly hot topics. In this climate, a theological synthesis is neither possible nor desirable, since such an achievement would greatly reduce the opportunities for making more money from a scandalized public. As a result they never get beyond soundings, explorations in theology and calls for reconstruction which, if they were ever answered, would be the death of their own mini growth industry.

The diachronically-based theologian must inevitably reject all behaviour of this kind, both because it is dilletantish and because it is un-Christian in its inspiration, for the process of selection extends also to historical tradition and the canonical texts, both of which are perverted in the interests of the dominant synchronic pressure. The diachronic theologian must preserve the integrity of both Scripture and tradition and respond to synchronic presssures by applying this integral understanding in a manner which is appropriate to the circumstances. His first task must be criticism of the present age in the light of the past; what is selected for inclusion in the ongoing tradition will be what has survived this searing investigation. In the nature of things it is not likely to be such, since few centuries leave any really large legacy behind them and the twentieth, which by all accounts appears to be an age of spiritual decline, may well be poorer than most. In the broad sweep of Christian tradition therefore, *sub specie aeternitatis* the church can only tolerate and absorb what is compatible with its own nature, a fact which at the present time is more likely to appear as a rejection of most, if not all, contemporary theological writing.

There is however, a fourth question which also must be asked, because of its bearing on the present situation. Is it possible to tolerate within the church, sub-systems of theology which may belong to particular groups or denominations but not to the whole? If it is, should we not view modern attempts to construct a basically synchronic, tolerant pluralism as the beginning of yet another sub-system which may one day take its place alongside the rest, or even be the model for a non-confessional, universal tradition of the future?

Traditions and Divisions

From the diachronic point of view, the different traditions of Christian theology developed out of disagreements which came to a head at particular moments in church history, when conflicting groups took different roads. The point at which they both intersect and divide is invariably the doctrine of the Trinity. All Christians are united because they confess the same trinitarian God and at the same time they are divided because they confess him in a different way - not at the level of liturgical practice only, but more importantly, at the level of doctrinal understanding. This can be illustrated by looking at the progress of the Christian church. Until the time of the Council of Chalcedon in 451, there was one church and one theology, deviations from which were carefully noted and condemned. At Chalcedon, the one true church broke up over the question, not of Christ's divinity but of his humanity. Nevertheless, because, as the Athanasian Creed puts it, Christ by his incarnation took manhood into God, this Christological issue became a theological question. The Chalcedonian Definition was a middle way between Nestorianism and Monophysitism drawn up by men who believed they were expressing the orthodox tradition of the one true church. But despite the anathemas, these movements continued to flourish and still exist - out of communion with the other churches, but not condemned by them, in the way that Unitarianism and Mormonism are. Even in ancient times there were attempts at reunion, and the schism did not become final until the Third Council of Constantinople in 680-681.

UNITY AND DIVERSITY IN CHRISTIAN THEOLOGY

The next division occurred in the Middle Ages, and concerned the procession of the Holy Spirit. The actual controversy began in the ninth century and was not finally concluded until the fifteenth - nearly six centuries later - but in spite of the many other factors which complicated the situation, the main outlines of the debate are clearly discernible. The third great division occurred in the sixteenth century, and concerned the work of the Holy Spirit above all else. It began with Luther's protest in 1517 and was complete at the latest by the end of the Council of Trent in 1563, though it took another century for its implications to be fully worked out.

In looking back over these divisions, two things are immediately apparent. The first is that they have occurred historically in an order which involves an ever narrower aspect of trinitarian theology. A refusal to believe in the Trinity itself is enough to produce a separate religion; a difference over the person of Christ puts both his work and the question of the Holy Spirit out of sight and a difference over the person of the Holy Spirit is enough to make the subsequent debates about his work seem incomprehensible. It is interesting to notice in this connection that although Protestants tend to regard Roman Catholics and Eastern Orthodox as virtually interchangeable because of their liturgical practices and ecclesiology (though they are by no means the same!), the Eastern Orthodox often see no real difference between Protestants and Roman Catholics, because they have no frame of reference in which to situate the arguments of the Reformation.

It is a paradox that differences which are closest to home and of least theological significance should be the ones which are most keenly felt. Protestants are generally much more anti-Catholic than anti-Orthodox, and it would be hard to find anybody who is anti-Nestorian or anti-Monophysite, even though on purely theological grounds there is much more reason to be such than to be anti-Catholic.

Another important point is that the divisions which have occurred were the result of long debate during the course of which the issues involved were fully aired. This has often been forgotten in the modern ecumenical movement, which sometimes pretends that theological traditions are so different now because they have evolved in isolation from one another. On the contrary, it is historically certain that they developed most rapidly in the glare of intense debate. When that cooled off and isolation was imposed, either by Islam or by the principle of *cuius regio, eius religio,* the different traditions fossilized and died. This happened to Protestant Orthodoxy in the seventeenth century when it was cut off from debate with Roman Catholicism, and the resulting stagnation paved the way for an abandonment of orthodoxy altogether when the new debating partner was Enlightenment rationalism, not the Church of Rome.

All this inevitably leads us to view theological sub-systems in a rather different light. They are not merely different ways of looking at the same thing; they have their origins in real debates which have taken place within the context of trinitarian theology. These debates were about issues which are still alive and about which one must still take a position, if one is truly trinitarian. It is because this perspective has been lost that it has become possible to regard the different traditions which have emerged from them as no more than regional or cultural variants of a single reality. Furthermore, it is only because modern theologians have so often abandoned the diachronic perspective that they have been able to ignore debates in trinitarian theology and have thought it possible to reconstruct a synchronic unity on the basis of a fundamental belief in the Trinity itself. To understand why this is impossible we must look more carefully at the precise points where the different traditions converge and diverge, for only in that way can we appreciate the logic which keeps them all alive, but apart.

UNITY AND DIVERSITY IN CHRISTIAN THEOLOGY

Unifying Factors

We come first of all to the unifying factors, which are basically three: first, the belief in a trinitarian God; second, the belief in the divinity of Jesus Christ; and third, the belief in the divine inspiration and central importance of Holy Scripture. Every authentic Christian theological tradition accepts these three key points. The last has been a matter of controversy and needs to be phrased carefully, but we must bear in mind that what we are agreed on is the nature of Scripture, not the scope of its authority, which in Catholic and Orthodox traditions is circumscribed, or supplemented, by other considerations.

It should also be pointed out that the inspiration of Scripture is a trinitarian question, not only because it is our only source for the doctrines of the Trinity, nor only because inspiration is the work of the Holy Spirit but also, and especially, because it is the Word of God, and the Word of God is Jesus Christ himself. The inspiration of Scripture is parallel to the incarnation of Christ, and the main lines of argument which appear in Christology are valid also for the doctrine of Scripture which is indwelt by the Holy Spirit.

It always seems difficult to talk at length about things of which we are agreed, but in fact there is a good deal to be said about the unifying factors in Christian theology. First of all, they are a good deal more restrictive than the kind of unity which James Dunn, for example, says was the norm in the early church. No Christian body today would accept that the mere confession 'Jesus is Lord' provides an adequate theological base, and every major church body subscribes to a series of beliefs which are not only more precise and more comprehensive than this, but which are held in common by all other major church bodies. This is highly significant because it shows that there is a Christian identity which transcends denominational barriers and which is sufficiently developed as a theological system to provide a common framework of discourse within which the different Christian traditions can function. It may be true that

69

no one tradition can be reduced to the common core material, but nor may it be regarded as no more than a point of view, or a way of receiving the common core. All traditions have extended and extrapolated from the common heritage in one way or another, but at the same time they have remained firmly rooted in the common core in a way which has made continuing dialogue and cross-fertilization possible. No doubt, as we hinted earlier, this very closeness has also had the opposite effect at times, by sharpening an awareness of differences and aggravating their impact on the church.

Nevertheless, the unifying factors in Christian theology retain their fundamental importance and provide a solid basis both for ecumenical discussion and for the further elaboration of existing traditions. If the latter are in some sense sub-systems of the whole, they are not fragments which have broken off the common core, or have simply dissolved the common core into nothing. It is therefore wrong to imagine that the proper response to the synchronic pressure for unity is to devise schemes for putting Humpty Dumpty together again, since such schemes are working with the wrong model in the first place. It is much better to think in terms of a branch-theory like the one put forward by Anglo-Catholics in the last century, but shorn of their particular bias. The trunk of the tree from which the branches have sprung cannot be equated either with the church of Rome or with the church of the early Christian centuries. It is not ecclesiological, but doctrinal, and the unity of the early church, such as it was, was only a unity on the fundamentals of the faith, which had to be clarified and protected against non-Christian pressures at work both within and without the body of the church. It also needs to be emphasized that if the church is like a tree, then the trunk and the branches will grow *together* but in different ways. The trunk will become more solid and more rooted in the soil in which it is planted, but its growth will be slow and be visible only over a period of time. The branches, on the other hand, will spread out and develop at a rate which is visibly faster, but which is always carefully balanced by the capacity of the trunk to support it.

Furthermore, if this model is accepted, it will be apparent that the ecumenical interest of the various branches will lie in making sure that nobody lays an axe to the root of the tree, for all will derive equal and essential nourishment from it. Naturally, this will have a considerable effect on the synchronic pressures for unity which govern official ecumenical discussion. These want to achieve unity by abolishing the branches by reintegrating them into the trunk of the tree. Modern ecumenism can accept cultural or regional diversity, but not ethological differences, which it regards as sapping the strength of the primordial trunk. Few stop to think that if this project were ever to be completed, the result would look more like a telegraph pole than a tree - or perhaps like a dead stump from which the branches have fallen off.

Not all proponents of modern ecumenism are theologically liberal, but that the two can go easily together is obvious, for a reduction of the branches to the trunk of the tree involves a deformation of the trunk. In the utilitarian, telegraph-pole model, which is peculiarly appropriate to a technological age, this deformation is also, necessarily, an uprooting of the tree from its native soil and its artificial planting, without roots, in a new and alien environment. This is what the liberal, synchronic pressures of our time are trying to achieve, and it is against this that the branches of the tree are called to struggle. We need to do this by emphasizing that the unity we have with other Christian traditions is present already, it does not have to be constructed or invented. We also need to stress that the healthiest way to promote it is to maintain and extend our diversity, drawing always on a common source and possibly becoming entwined with other branches at different points along the way, but never losing the strength or individuality which gives each branch its particular beauty and importance.

If this perspective can be communicated to the Evangelical world it may have the double effect of opening it to the influence

Gerald Bray

of other Christian traditions without in any way minimizing or detracting from its own integrity and purpose.

Divisive Factors

Having established both the importance and the possible role of the unifying factors in Christian theology, we are now compelled to take a closer look at the things which divide us. At the lowest level of the tree-trunk, if we stick to that image, there are the branches which have gone their own way because of differences concerning the person and work of Jesus Christ. Neither the Nestorians nor the Monophysites were able to hold the divinity and the humanity of Jesus in the proper balance, even though both were motivated in this by a concern, shared with the great church, that the work of Christ should be preserved in its fulness. The branches were therefore formed by people whose heart was in the right place but who, for that very reason, felt compelled to take a different direction in theology. Nestorianism, which overemphasizes the humanity of Christ, is the exact counterpart of Monophysitism, which overemphasizes his divinity - the two branches counterbalance each other.

In the early centuries, when they were virtually the only branches which existed, they developed and prospered but, as so often happens with the lower branches of a tree, they gradually stopped growing and even began to shed some of their fruit. They were near enough to the ground to be an easy target for non-Christian predators, and both succumbed to the pressures of Islam. Today, though they still exist, they are but a shadow of their former selves, and are as susceptible to outside pressures as they have ever been.

Farther up the tree we come to the first major split in the trunk itself - that which occurred over the question of the procession of the Holy Spirit. To many people this may appear to be less important than the earlier Christological controversies, but in fact it is more serious than they were. In the earlier case, the

72

substance of the matter was agreed on all sides, and only the formulations differed. In the dispute about the procession of the Holy Spirit the substance itself was a matter of controversy, which even an agreed formulation, like that of the Council of Florence in 1439, could do nothing to overcome. This needs to be said with great clarity, because one of the major problems which confronts students of the *Filioque* dispute today is the common conviction among western scholars - most, but not all of them liberals - that it is a debate about words which has no substance. On the contrary, it is in fact a major cleavage which has repercussions at every level of church life. The reason for this is simply that the Holy Spirit is the founder of the church and the person of the Trinity most directly involved in its preservation on earth. It is not too much to say that in a very real sense, he is our contact-point with God. It is he who makes our adoption as sons in Christ a reality, and he who empowers us to pray to the Father.

It is therefore of crucial importance for us to know just how he is related to the two persons whom he unites us with, since we can scarcely be united with them in a way which is different from his union with them. The Western Church argues that the Holy Spirit is related equally and in the same way to both the Father and the Son. The Eastern Church argues that the Holy Spirit is related to the Father in a way which is more fundamental than his relationship to the Son, but leaves open the question of what the latter relationship consists in. This difference of theology is bound to have its effect on the life of the church, especially when the work of the Holy Spirit is being considered. Time and again we discover that differences which have occurred within the Western Church on this issue simply have no counterpart in the Eastern Church, and Eastern theologians are often at a loss to understand what the problems are. Many see little difference between Protestants and Catholics, because they have divided from the Western Church *as a whole* and therefore tend to perceive it as a unity even today. This is one reason why Protestants and Orthodox, in spite of many shared beliefs, particularly with regard to the

Roman Church and its authority, have never moved closer to one another in practical terms.

It is interesting to note that the split in the Western Church did not begin until the split between East and West had become definitive; indeed, the two events are almost contemporaneous. Curiously enough, the same was also true of the beginning of the East-West split, which followed hard on the final separation of Nestorians and Monophysites. It is almost as if there is a pause for breath when each split is consummated, before the continuing process of division begins again.

In any event, the sixteenth-century split between Protestants and Roman Catholics occurred primarily over issues which are directly linked to the work of the Holy Spirit. It is one of the curiosities of theological history that this simple fact is seldom correctly perceived, even by those who are most familiar with the subject. Depending on who you ask, the explanation which will be given for the Reformation will range from the corruption of the medieval church, to the rediscovery of the doctrine of justification by faith alone, the rejection of papal authority and the claims of Renaissance science. Of course, all these factors were involved, but what gives coherence to the movement as a whole is the understanding of the work of the Holy Spirit – a fact which is borne out by countless Reformation treatises on that subject, and by the fact – which seems slightly curious to our generation – that no less a figure than Calvin himself has always been known as the theologian of the Holy Spirit.

If we return to popular impressions as given above, what do we find when we apply this principle? First, we discover that the church, in the mind of the Reformers, is the invisible community of the Spirit rather than the visible body of Christ. It is the confirmation of Pentecost, not the incarnation, as Roman Catholic ecclesiology likes to have it. A Catholic can say, as many have in fact said, that the Son of God came to earth and *left behind* the church; a Protestant would say that the

Son of God ascended into heaven and sent his Holy Spirit to create the church – a rather different thing!

In the matter of justification by faith alone we are really dealing with the broader issue of how the Spirit works in the life of the believer. The Catholic argues that it is by mediated grace, possessed and conveyed by the church with its priests and sacraments. The Protestant argues that it is by immediate grace; the Holy Spirit speaks directly to our hearts, giving us the faith to believe that we have been justified by Christ's atoning sacrifice. In both ways of thinking, grace is a work of the Holy Spirit, but in the Catholic scheme the Spirit first sanctifies *things* – water, bread and wine – which are then applied to *people,* whereas in the Protestant case, the Holy Spirit sanctifies only people. The outward signs, though important and helpful, possess no virtue in and of themselves.

The people-centred, rather than thing-centred emphasis of Protestantism can be seen right across the whole spectrum of devotional life. Protestants put preaching the gospel before all else, and reject extreme forms of sacramental piety. Protestants emphasize the importance of individual witness, whereas Roman Catholics stress the corporate dimension, as in the so-called religious life. Protestants emphasize the responsibility which each Christian has in the sight of God; Roman Catholics interpose the ministry of a confessor-priest, not as is often thought, in his individual capacity, but as the voice of the church (which is why such efforts are made to preserve the anonymity of the confessional), and so on. Enough has been said to give the general gist of the argument.

As for the papacy, the difference of opinion begins with the simple question – who is the vicar of Christ on earth? For Roman Catholics, the answer is obvious – the pope. For Protestants, the answer is equally obvious – the Holy Spirit, that other Comforter whom the Father has sent in Christ's name. The question of authority, or jurisdiction, naturally flows from this. Protestant churches recognize only the authority of the Holy Spirit, as this has been revealed in the Scriptures. Roman Catholics accept that the Bible is a book inspired by the Holy Spirit, but place their authority in the pope, who has the right to make infallible doctrinal pronouncements which may or may not have scriptural support. In case of doubt, moreover, it is the word of the pope, not that of the Bible, which takes precedence. In this context, it should be said that many people argue that Roman authority really resides in the church, of which the pope is only the privileged spokesman. That was certainly the legal position until 1870, and since Vatican II it has been revived by many ecumenically-minded Catholics. Yet the fact of the matter is that the papacy continues to extend its very unique authority, and that many Catholics look to it to enforce or correct the teaching of the Church given by other bodies, such as councils and papal commissions. This authority has recently been powerfully supported by the mass-media, where the pope inevitably steals the show. In a very real sense, therefore, the position of the vicar of Christ has been greatly reinforced in modern Catholicism, and this is the logical extension of earlier tendencies. It is also the logical counterpart of *sola Scriptura,* sometimes disparagingly – but not altogether inaccurately – referred to as a 'paper pope' by those who would prefer to dispense with its authority altogether. Here as elsewhere, we must see beyond the smokescreen of ecumenical propaganda and consider what the reality is – something very different indeed from what most people imagine!

Lastly, there is the question of Renaissance science. Rome silenced Galileo and later tried to resurrect the philosophy of Thomas Aquinas as its guiding light in the modern world. The general result of its efforts has been academic stagnation, even in theology, from which only secularization and Protestant influence have rescued it. The Reformers, on the other hand, generally welcomed the new learning because they believed that the Holy Spirit could, and did, speak to man outside the bounds of the worship of the visible church. They declared that secular callings were holy, that a scientist engaged in research was uncovering the secret beauty of God's own handiwork. If it is true that they sometimes had a naive faith in scientists which was readily shattered when the latter turned out to be heretics and unbelievers in large numbers, this too must be explained primarily by their failure to apply their principle that the Holy Spirit works in *people*, not in things or theories, to the realm of science and the other secular callings. In our own time, when we have proved that the devil can use technology to great effect, this truth is slowly and painfully being rediscovered – we can only hope, before it is too late!

This, then, is a brief sketch of the Protestant-Roman Catholic theological divide. Within the Protestant world there are further divisions, though as I said at the beginning of this paper, these tend to be ecclesiological rather than theological – a direction which makes sense in the context of Protestant teaching about the work of the Spirit, in which ecclesiastical structures are often thought to be of secondary importance. Indeed, it is highly significant that the modern ecumenical movement began as a Protestant, spiritual attempt to achieve unity above and beyond denominational barriers. Only since the 1920s has the original movement diverged into conservative Evangelicals, who have discovered and generally maintained this unity in a series of interdenominational organizations, and liberal Evangelicals, who have devoted themselves to denominational mergers, ecumenical discussions and even inter-faith dialogue.

Splits over Scripture

Mention of liberals and conservatives within the Protestant camp brings us to the last, and for many the most painful of all the splits which have occurred within the Church. This is the split over the inspiration and authority of Holy Scripture. Just as the Protestant-Catholic divide makes little sense to Orthodox Christians, who view the issues in quite a different perspective, the liberal-conservative divide within Protestantism is also often misunderstood by outsiders. Other Christians treat the authority of Scripture very differently, and though they accept its divine inspiration are seldom bothered by the details. Only in the context of a theological tradition whose authority is the voice of the Holy Spirit can the question of where that voice is to be heard assume crucial practical importance. Because traditional Protestantism asserted that it could be heard only in Scripture, which thus became the final authority for the Church, the question of the text's inspiration and status cannot be avoided in Protestant theology.

At first sight, it must be said that the liberal position looks more plausible, because it appears to continue the development of Protestantism in a more radical way, shedding some of conservative Evangelicalism's catholic hangovers – the credal framework of doctrine, the inspiration of Scripture and so on. In particular, its strongest claim is that God speaks to and through people, not things – and the Bible is a thing! It is often supposed, moreover, that liberalism can only be a thinly-veiled rationalism with little or no connection with the main body of the church at the level of worshipping congregations. But, in reality, this is far from being the case. Liberalism is rampant in the churches, and very enthusiastic indeed. Intellectually, it appears as Barthian neo-orthodoxy; devotionally, it is most evident in the charismatic movement. Put the two together, as is happening more and more today, and you have a powerful, seemingly orthodox theology based ultimately on subjective experience, not on objective inspiration.

It may seem very odd to say that charismatics are liberals, when so many seem to be ultra-conservative in doctrinal matters, but this conservatism is really an illusion. In practice, charismatics show a theological indifference which makes the World Council of Churches look almost sectarian. If you speak in tongues you are 'in', regardless of what you might believe in other areas. The movement is characterized by a divorce between spirit and reason which is the very essence of romantic liberalism and takes us right back to the eighteenth century. It puts an emphasis on personal experience which is so central that academic study appears to be not only unnecessary, but even diabolical by comparison. Like more traditional Evangelicals, charismatics revolt against the rationalistic theology of our universities, but whereas the former strive to provide something better, the latter ignore it altogether, preferring to derive their own blessed thoughts from the Bible. If this Bible reading ever becomes serious Bible study, the charismatic reader is left exposed to the most radical forms of liberal thought which he may piece together in a quite disorganized way. Let a doubter read one of James Dunn's more recent books, if he needs to be convinced of this.

The debate about Scripture is by no means over in Protestant circles, and although some groups and organizations belong clearly on one side of the fence or another, most are still trying to sit on it – including the major denominations. Broadly speaking, the situation is that paper confessions and the like favour the conservatives, whilst actual interpretations are so broad that they favour the liberals. This has been true in the main denominations for about a century now, and it is beginning to creep into organizations originally set up by conservatives to combat this earlier trend. On the other hand, modern conservatives have organized their theological resources to fight back – most notably in the Chicago Declaration of Inerrancy, published in 1978. This document, whose ultimate historical importance is still unknown, is the most important statement to date of a reasoned conservative position. If it is weak in some places, it is probably because little attempt has been made to set it in the context of the wider theological issues which have been raised in this paper. If we believe, as we presumably do, that God speaks to people, how are we going to relate what the Bible says to what God is saying to us? Does he just explain what the words mean, as a kind of heavenly encyclopaedia of information, or does he interpret these for us in our situation today? Most Evangelicals will opt for the latter, but in that case, how do we avoid the crypto-liberalism of the New Hermeneutic? It is not much good having an inspired text if nobody can understand it, or if the understanding is subject to changing scholarly opinion and/or spiritual fashions.

The answer to this problem, I think, needs to be found in a new understanding of tradition as person-to-person contact through the ages – the communion of saints who since apostolic times have lived, preached and handed on the gospel. Even more, we need to insist that in the Bible we have the *living voice* of the Spirit and not merely the historical record of what he once said. The interpretation of this living voice must once again be seen to belong to the preacher, whose gift it properly is, and not to the scholar, whose disciplines are secondary and auxiliary to the main task. Whether the Evangelical world, which is as dominated by scholars as is any other part of the church, is really up to the task remains to be seen. It may well be that there will be further and greater divisions before this common understanding can be reached.

We have come then, by a somewhat lengthy route, to the burning issues of the present day. As in the past, the pain of separation is not caused by the things which divide us – on these we have perhaps never been in contact – but on the things which continue to unite us, but which are powerless to prevent further division. Liberal and conservative Protestants share many things in common. Moreover, until the final separation takes place – and that, as we have seen, will happen only after centuries of debate during which a precise theological platform,. excluding the alternatives, will have been worked out – there will be a grey area of people who will float from one side to the other, and both groups will continue to work together at many different levels. These things have to be expected – it was the same at the time of the Reformation, the same in the Middle Ages, the same in the early church – but the general sense of movement should also be expected, and understood!

Conclusion

In conclusion therefore, I want to say that Christian theology has a fundamental unity which its many traditions share in differing degrees. The diversity which has manifested itself over the centuries has proceeded logically from one theological point to the next. However strong political or cultural factors may have been in promoting the various divisions, the fundamental motive has always been a theological one. Only that can adequately explain the enduring character of the divisions and the resistance which they have shown to subsequent attempts at reunion.

The church today is perhaps best compared to a tree, its various branches mingling with each other in different ways and touching each other at different points, so that seen from certain angles they might even appear to be one. But in reality the branches cannot be cut down without destroying the tree, nor can the trunk do any more than continue to feed their growth, in the process growing slowly itself. As is the way with such things, the tree's beauty can only be perceived at a distance. The view from any one of the branches is complicated and may even be off-putting. Yet I believe that God, in his good time, will take us up from those branches and give us, not the tree of theology, but the tree of life whose leaves are for the healing of the nations – the presence and power of Jesus Christ himself, enthroned in his glory in heaven.

THE JUSTIFICATION OF THEOLOGY

With a Special Application to Contemporary Christology

ROBERT L. REYMOND

The highly esteemed American philosopher-theologian of revered and recent memory, Dr Gordon Haddon Clark, begins his 1984 book, *In Defense of Theology*, with the following statement:

> Theology, once acclaimed 'the Queen of the Sciences,' today hardly rises to the rank of a scullery maid; it is often held in contempt, regarded with suspicion, or just ignored.[1]

If Professor Clark is correct in his assessment, that is to say, if there is today this widespread disregard bordering on contempt for theology, one might at first blush be excused if he should feel it entirely proper to be done with theology altogether and to devote his time and energies to some intellectual pursuit holding out promise of higher esteem among men. One might even wonder wherein resides the justification for such a gathering as this, called for the express purpose of advancing the cause of theology. The issue can be pointedly framed in the form of a question: How is theology,[2] as an intellectual discipline deserving today of the church's highest interest and of the occupation of men's minds, to be justified?

---

1. *In Defense of Theology*, Milford, Michigan, 1984, p. 3.
2. The term 'theology' is used in this paper in the somewhat restricted but still fairly broad sense for the disciplines of the classical divinity curriculum with its departments of exegetical, historical, systematic, and practical theology, or for what is practically the same thing, namely, the intelligent effort which seeks to understand the Bible, viewed as revealed truth, as a coherent whole.

THE JUSTIFICATION OF THEOLOGY

If this conference were a conference in philosophical theology, to this question I would respond with one very simple basic sentence: God has revealed truth about himself, about us, and about the relationship between himself and us in Holy Scripture; therefore, we should study Holy Scripture.

The product of such study would be theology. Or we might say this another way: if there is a God, he must be someone we should know; and if he has spoken to us in and by the Scriptures of the Old and New Testaments, that very fact is sufficient warrant in itself to justify our study of the Scriptures. Indeed, it mandates the study of Scripture, or what amounts to the same thing, the engagement of men in the theological enterprise. We would even urge that not to study Scripture, *if God has revealed himself therein* , is the height of folly and the clearest evidence of a certain kind of insanity!

This particular ground or justification for the study of theology is so overwhelming that all other reasons, from an apologetic perspective, would be unnecessary. And I say again, if this were a conference in philosophical theology or apologetics, that this would be the justification I would offer for doing theology. Then the remainder of this paper would be devoted to the task of stating the case for what has often been called the first principle of the Christian faith, namely, that God is 'really there' and that he has spoken to us, rationally, authoritatively, and univocally, in and by the inspired Scriptures of his prophets and apostles. This task I have already attempted to do in my book on apologetic method, entitled *The Justification of Knowledge,* [3] so I see no need to restate the entire case now. Suffice it to say simply at this point that, for me, the Scriptures of the Old and New Testaments are self-arrestingly, self-authenticatingly of divine origin as to content and message, the Word of the self-attesting Christ of Scripture, carrying inherently within them their own divine *indicia*, such as

---

3. Robert L. Reymond, *The Justification of Knowledge*, Phillipsburg, New Jersey, 1984.

 Reymond

the heavenliness of the matter, the efficacy of the doctrine, the majesty of the style, the consent of all the parts, the scope [goal] of the whole (which is to give all glory to God), the full discovery [disclosure] it makes of the only way of man's salvation, the many other incomparable excellencies, and the entire perfection thereof (*Westminster Confession of Faith*, I,v),

which properties, the *Confession of Faith* also reminds us, are 'arguments whereby [the Holy Scripture] doth *abundantly evidence* itself to be the Word of God' (I,v; emphasis supplied). If my concern today, may I say once again, were purely and strictly an apologetic one, it would be Augustinian/Anselmic/Calvinistic fideism, or perhaps more simply phrased, biblical presuppositionalism, expressed in the phrase *'credo ut intelligam'* ('I believe in order that I may understand'), wherein the child of God through *believing* study seeks an ever-fuller *understanding*[4] of the self-authenticating truth of God in Scripture, which I would urge and defend.

The nature of this conference, it seems to me, however, calls for the explication of a different kind of rationale for engaging in the theological enterprise, and this I would suggest should be done along lines more biblical than apologetical.

The Biblical Justification for Theology

When we inquire into the issue before this dogmatics conference on the justification of theology, if I understand its intended import, what we are asking is simply this: Why should we engage ourselves in intellectual and scholarly reflection on the message and content of Holy Scripture? And a related question is this: Why do we do this, as Christians, the particular way that we do? To these questions, I would suggest, the New Testament offers at least the following four reasons: (1) Christ's own theological method, (2) Christ's mandate to teach

---

4.   *Fides quaerens intellectum.*

84

in the Great Commission, (3) the apostolic model, and (4) the apostolically-approved example and activity of the New Testament church. Consider each of these briefly with me.

Christ's Own Theological Method

It is Christ himself, by his example of appealing to Scripture and by his method of interpretation, who established for his church both the prerogative and the pattern to exegete the Scriptures of the Old and New Testaments in the special way that she does, and to derive from those Scriptures, by theological deduction, their special application to his person and work. This is clear from the New Testament itself. For in addition to those specific occasions when he applied the Old Testament to himself (cf., for example, Matt.22:41-45; Luke 4:14-21; John 5:46), we are informed in Luke 24:25-27 that 'beginning with Moses and all the prophets, (the glorified Christ) *explained* [*diermeneusen*] to them in all the Scriptures the things concerning himself' (emphasis supplied). Beyond all controversy, such an exhaustive engagement in Scripture exposition involved our Lord in theological activity in the most heightened sense. In his small book, *According to the Scriptures*, with great sensitivity and depth of insight, C.H. Dodd develops the point I am making here. Let us listen to this eminent biblical scholar for a few moments:

> At the earliest period of Church history to which we can gain access,we find in being the rudiments of an original, coherent and flexible method of biblical exegesis which was already beginning to yield results.

> ... Very diverse scriptures are brought together so that they interpret one another in hitherto unsuspected ways. To have brought together, for example, the Son of Man who is the people of the saints of the Most High, the Man of God's right hand, who is also the vine of Israel, the Son of Man who after humiliation is crowned with glory and honour, and the victorious priest-king at the

right hand of God, is an achievement of interpretative imagination which results in the creation of an entirely new figure. It involves an original, and far-reaching, resolution of the tension between the individual and the collective aspects of several of these figures, which in turn makes it possible to bring into single focus the 'plot' of the Servant poems ... , of the psalms of the righteous sufferer, and of the prophecies of the fall and recovery (death and resurrection) of the people of God, and finally offers a fresh understanding of the mysterious imagery of apocalyptic eschatology.

This is a piece of genuinely creative thinking. Who was responsible for it?   The early Church, we are accustomed to say, ... But creative thinking is rarely done by committees, useful as they may be for systematizing the fresh ideas of individual thinkers, and for stimulating them to further thought. It is individual minds that originate. Whose was the originating mind here?

Among Christian thinkers of the first age known to us there are three of genuinely creative power: Paul, the author to the Hebrews, and the Fourth Evangelist. We are precluded from proposing any one of them for the honour of having originated the process, since even Paul, greatly as he contributed to its development, demonstrably did not originate it ... the New Testament itself avers that it was Jesus Christ himself who first directed the minds of his followers to certain parts of the scriptures as those in which they might find illumination upon the meaning of his mission and destiny ... I can see no reasonable ground for rejecting the statements of the Gospels that (for example) he pointed to Psalm cx as a better guide to the truth about his mission and destiny than the popular beliefs about the Son of David, or that ·he made that connection of the 'Lord' at God's right hand with the Son of Man in Daniel which proved so momentous for Christian thought, or that he associated with the Son of Man language which had been used of the Servant of the Lord, and employed it to hint at the meaning, and the issue, of his own approaching death. To account for the beginning of this most original and fruitful process of rethinking the Old Testament we found need to postulate a creative mind. The Gospels offer us one.[5]

Beyond dispute the Gospels depict Jesus of Nazareth as entering deeply into the engagement of mind with Scripture and drawing out original and fascinating theological deductions therefrom. And it is he who establishes for us the pattern and end of our own theologizing - the pattern: we must follow him in making the exposition of Scripture the basis of our theology; and the end: we must arrive finally at *him* in all of our theological labours.

The Mandate in the Great Commission

Theology is a mandated task of the church; of this there can be no doubt. For after setting for us the example and establishing for us the pattern and end of all theology, the glorified Christ commissioned his church to *teach (didaskontes)* all nations (Matt.28:18-20). And theology, essential to this teaching, serves in carrying out the Great Commission as it seeks to set forth in a logical and coherent manner the truth God has revealed in Holy Scripture about himself and the world he has created.

---

5. C.H. Dodd, *According to the Scriptures*, London, 1952, pp. 108-110. One caveat is in order here, however. While we obviously appreciate Dodd's granting to Jesus alone the creative genius to bring these several Old Testament themes together to enhance understanding of His person and work, it is extremely important to insist that, in doing so, Jesus did not bring a meaning to the Old Testament that was not intrinsic to the Old Testament itself. *Cf.* also Gerald Bray, *Creeds, Councils and Christ*, Downers Grove, Illinois, 1984, p. 50.

The divine commission to the church to disciple, baptize, and teach all nations clearly places upon the church, indwelt and empowered by the Holy Spirit, certain *intellectual* demands. There is the *evangelistic* demand to address the gospel to the needs of every generation, for the commission is to disciple all the nations, with no restriction as to time and place. There is the *didactic* (or catechetic) demand 'to correlate the manifold data of revelation in our understanding and the more effectively apply this knowledge to all phases of our thinking and conduct.'[6] Finally, there is, as we have already noted, the apologetic (or polemic) demand ultimately to justify the existence of Christianity and to protect the message of Christianity from adulteration and distortion (cf. Tit.1:9). Theology has risen, and properly so, in the life of the church in response to these concrete demands in fulfilling the Great Commission.

The Apostolic Model

Such activity as eventually led to the church's engagement in theology is found not only in the teaching of Jesus Christ but also in the rest of the New Testament. Paul wastes no time after his baptism in his effort to 'prove' (*sumbibazon)* to his fellow Jews that Jesus is the Christ (Acts 9:22). Later, as a seasoned missionary, he enters the synagogue in Thessalonica 'and on three Sabbath days he *reasoned* [*dielexato,* 'dialogued'] with them *from the Scriptures* , *explaining* [*dianoigon*] and *proving* [*paratithemenos*] that Christ had to suffer and rise from the dead' (Acts 17:2-3; emphasis supplied). The learned Apollos 'vigorously *refuted* [*diakatelencheto*] the Jews in public debate, *proving* [*epideiknus*] *from the Scriptures* that Jesus was the Christ' (Acts 18:28; emphasis supplied).

---

6.   John Murray, 'Systematic Theology', *Westminster Theological Journal* 25 (1963), p. 138.

Nor is Paul's evangelistic 'theologizing' limited to the synagogue. While waiting for Silas and Timothy in Athens Paul 'reasoned [*dielegetol*] in the synagogue with the Jews and the God-fearing Greeks, as well as *in the market-place* day by day with those who happened to be there' (Acts 17:17); emphasis supplied). This got him an invitation to address the Areopagus which he did in terms that could be understood by the Epicurean and Stoic philosophers gathered there (cf. his quotation from the Greek poets in 17:27), without, however, any accommodation of his message to what they were prepared to believe. In a masterful theological summary presented with evangelistic and apologetic sensitivity, Paul carefully presented the great truths of revelation concerning the Creator, man created in his image, and man's need to come to God through the Judge and Saviour he has provided, even Jesus Christ.

But Paul's 'theologizing' was not exclusively evangelistic. In addition to that three-month period at Ephesus during which he spoke boldly in the synagogue, arguing persuasively *(dialegomenos kai peithon)* about the kingdom of God (Acts 19:8), Paul had discussions *(dialegomenos)* daily in the lecture hall of Tyrannus over a two-year period, not hesitating, as he was to say later (cf. Acts 20:17-35). 'to preach anything that would be helpful to you but have taught [*didaxai*] you publicly and from house to house,' declaring to both Jews and Greeks that they must turn to God in repentance and have faith in Jesus Christ (Acts 20:20-21). In a word, he declares: 'I have not hesitated to proclaim the *whole will of God'* (Acts 20:27; emphasis supplied).

No doubt we see in the epistle to the Romans, Paul's major exposition of the message entrusted to him, not only the broad outline and essential content of the gospel Paul preached but also the theologizing method he employed. Notice should be taken here of the theological flow of the letter: how Paul moves logically and systematically from the plight of the human condition to God's provision of salvation in Christ, then, in turn, on to the results of justification, objections to the doctrine, and finally to the Christian ethic that results from God's mercies towards us.   It detracts in no way from Paul's 'inspiredness' (1 Thes. 2:13; 2 Pet. 3:15-16; 2 Tim. 3:16) to acknowledge, as he set forth this theological flow of thought under the Spirit's superintendence, that he reflected upon, and deduced theological conclusions from (1) earlier inspired conclusions, (2) biblical history, and (3) even his own personal position in Christ. Indeed, one finds these 'theologizing reflections and deductions' embedded in the very heart of some of the apostle's most radical assertions.   For example, after stating certain propositions, at least ten times Paul asks: 'What shall we say [conclude] then?'   and proceeds to 'deduce by good and necessary consequence' the conclusion he desires his reader to reach (cf. 3:5, 9; 4:1; 6:1, 15; 7:7; 8:31; 9:14, 30; 11:7).   In the fourth chapter the apostle draws the theological conclusion both that circumcision is unnecessary to the blessing of justification and that Abraham is the spiritual father of the uncircumcised Gentile believer from the simple observation based on Old Testament history that 'Abraham believed the Lord, and he credited it to him for righteousness' (Gen.15:6) some fourteen years *before* he was circumcised (Gen.17:24) – striking theological deductions, to say the least, to draw in his particular religious and cultural milieu simply from the 'before and after' relationship between two historical events.   Later, to prove that 'at the present time there is a remnant chosen by grace' (Rom.11:5), Paul simply appeals to his own status as a Christian Jew (Rom.11:2), again a striking assertion to derive from the simple fact of his own faith in Jesus.   Surely the apostolic model lends its weight to the point I am making respecting the justification of our engagement in the enterprise.

The Activity of the New Testament Church

Finally, our engagement in the task and formation of theology as an intellectual discipline based upon and derived from Scripture gains additional support from the obvious activity of the New Testament church itself,[7] for our attention is again and again already called in the New Testament to a body of saving truth, as in Jude 3 ('the faith once delivered to the saints'), 1 Timothy 6:20 ('the deposit), 2 Thessalonians 2:15 ('the traditions'), Romans 6:17 ('the pattern of doctrine'), and the 'faithful sayings' of the pastoral letters of Paul (1 Tim. 1:15; 3:1; 4:8-9; 2 Tim. 2:11-13; Tit. 3:3-8).[8] These descriptive terms and phrases unmistakably and incontestably indicate that in the days of the apostles the theologizing process of reflecting upon and comparing Scripture with Scripture, collating, deducing, and framing doctrinal statements into creedal formulae approaching the character of church confessions had already begun (cf. for examples of these creedal formulae Rom. 10:9; 1 Cor. 12:3; 1 Tim. 3:16). And all of this was done with the full knowledge and approval of the apostles, indeed, with the full and personal engagement and involvement of the apostles themselves in the theologizing process (cf., for example, in Acts 15:1-16:5 the activity of the apostles in the Jerusalem assembly, labouring not only as apostles but also as elders in the deliberative activity of preparing a conciliar theological response to the issue being considered then for the church's guidance).

Hence, when we today, under the guidance of the Spirit of God and in faith, come to Holy Scripture and with all the best intellectual tools make an effort to explicate it, trace its workings in the world, systematize its teachings, formulate its teachings into creeds, and propagate its message, thus hard won, to the world, we are standing squarely in the theologizing process present in and witnessed and mandated by the New Testament itself!

---

7.   *Cf.* J. N. D. Kelly, 'Creedal Elements in the New Testament', *Early Christian Creeds*, London, 1950.
8.   *Cf.* George W. Knight, III, *The Faithful Sayings in the Pastoral Letters*, Kampen, 1968.

Surely herein resides the biblical justification for the theological enterprise in our own time and our personal engagement in it. Indeed, so clear is the scriptural mandate for theology that one is not speaking to excess were he to suggest that our concern should not be one primarily of whether we should *engage* ourselves in theology or not - the Lord of the church and his apostles leave us no other option here (cf. Matt. 28:20; 2 Tim. 2:2; Tit. 1:9; 2:1); we have to be engaged in it if we are going to be faithful to him. Rather, what should be of greater concern to us is whether, in our engagement, we are *listening* as intently and submissively as we should to his voice speaking to his church in Holy Scripture. In short, our primary concern should be: Is our theology correct? Or perhaps better: Is it orthodox?

A Case In Point: Two Modern Christologies

An illustration that, for me, highlights this greater concern is what is being written today in the area of Christology. Such writing justifies in a powerful way the place for continuing engagement in orthodox theology. Just as the central issue of church theology in the Book of Acts was christological (cf. 9:22; 17:2-3; 18:28), so also today Christ's own questions, 'What do you think about the Christ? Whose son is he?' (Matt. 22:42), continue to occupy centre stage in current theological debate. While the conciliar decision of Chalcedon in A.D. 451 espousing a two-natured Christ has generally satisfied Christian orthodoxy, it has fallen upon hard times in the church in our day (*cf.* for example, an extreme example of this in *The Myth of God Incarnate*). The church dogma that this one Lord Jesus Christ is very God and very man and is both of these in the full unabridged sense of these terms and is both of these at the same time has been increasingly rejected, not only, it is alleged, on biblical grounds but also as a contradiction, an impossibility, indeed, a rank absurdity. As a result, it is widely affirmed today that Christology in a way heretofore unparalleled in the church is simply 'up for grabs.' It is 'a whole new ball game.'

THE JUSTIFICATION OF THEOLOGY

The Johannine phrase, *ho logos sarx egeneto*, is at the centre of the modern debate and in its own way, as a point of departure, crystallizes the major issue of the current debate: Is Christology to be a Christology 'from below,' that is, is it to take its starting point in a human Jesus *(sarx)* or is it to be a Christology 'from above,' that is, is it to begin with the Son of God *(ho logos)* come to us from heaven? And in either case, what precisely is the import of John's choice of verbs: the *egeneto*? Faced with such questions, is it not clear that never has the need been greater for careful, biblically-governed, hermeneutically-meticulous theologizing as the church addresses the perennial question: *Who is Jesus of Nazareth*?

Any response to this question would be well-advised to recall at the outset that the ultimate aim of the early Fathers throughout the decades of controversy over this matter (A.D. 325-451) was simply to describe and to defend the verbal picture which the Gospels and the rest of the New Testament draw of Jesus of Nazareth. Certainly there were the party strife and the personal rancour between some individuals which made complete objectivity in the debate extremely difficult at times. But a faithful reading of the Nicene and post-Nicene Fathers must lead one to the conclusion that neither was it the concern just to 'have it one's own way' on the part of those engaged in the debate nor was it the desire to contrive a doctrinal formula so intellectually preposterous that it would be a stumbling block to all but the most gullible of men that led them to speak as they did of Jesus Christ as a two-natured single person. Rather, what ultimately underlay their entire effort, we may affirm without fear of correction, was simply the faithful (that is, 'full of faith') resolve to·set forth as accurately as words available to them could do what the New Testament said about Jesus. If their creedal terms were sometimes the terms of earlier and current philosophy, those terms nonetheless served the church well then and still do in most quarters of the Christian community in communicating who the Bible declares Jesus to be. If the 'four great Chalcedonian adverbs' *(asunkutos* [without confusion], *atreptos* [without change or transmutation], *adiairetos* [without division], *achoristos* [without separation or contrast]) describe not so much how the two natures – the human and the divine – *are* to be related to each other in the unity of the one person of Christ as how they *are not* to be related, again it can and should be said that these adverbs served to protect both what the Fathers believed the Scriptures clearly taught about Jesus and, at the same time, the *mystery* of his person as well. My own deep longing is that the church today might be as faithful and perceptive in assessing the picture of Jesus in the Gospels for our time as these spiritual forebears were for theirs.

I fear, however, that it is not just a modern dissatisfaction with their usage of Greek philosophical terminology or the belief that the early Fathers simply failed to read the Bible as accurately as they might have that lies behind the totally new and different reconstructions of Jesus presently being produced by doctors in the church. Rather, it is a new and foreign manner of reading the New Testament, brought in by the 'assured results' of 'Enlightenment criticism' - a new hermeneutic reflecting canons of interpretation neither derived from Scripture nor sensitive to grammatical/historical rules of reading an ancient text - that is leading men to draw totally new portraits of Christ; but along with these new portraits of Christ, a Christ also emerges whose purpose is no longer to reverse the effects of a space/time fall from an original state of integrity and to bring men in to the supernatural kingdom of God and eternal life, but rather to shock the modern somehow into an existentially-conceived 'authentic existence,' or into any number of other religio-psychological responses to him.

Now I believe that it is quite in order to ask, over against the creators of these 'new Christs': Is the mind-set of modern man really such that he is incapable of believing in the Chalcedonian Christ and the so-called 'mythological kerygma' (Bultmann) of the New Testament? Is it so that modern science compels the necessity of 'demythologizing' the church's proclamation and to reinterpret it existentially? I believe not. In fact, what I find

94

truly amazing is just how many truly impossible things (more than seven, I assure you) modern man is able to believe every day - such as the view that asserts that this present universe is the result of an impersonal beginning out of nothing, plus time plus chance, or that man is the result solely of forces latent within nature itself, or that man is essentially good and morally perfectible through education and social manipulation, or that justice and morals need not be grounded in ethical absolutes.

It is also still in order to ask: Who has better read and more carefully handled the biblical material - the ancient or the new Christologist - with reference to both the person and the purpose of Jesus Christ?

Bultmann's Existential Jesus

Consider Bultmann, the exegete, for a moment as a case in point. When, in his commentary on John he comes to John 1:14, he writes: 'The Logos became flesh! It is the *language of mythology* that is here employed,'[9] specifically 'the mythological language of Gnosticism.'[10] For Bultmann, all emphasis in this statement falls on *sarx* and its meaning, so that 'the Revealer is nothing but a man.'[11] Moreover, the Revealer's *doxa* 'is not to be seen ... *through* the *sarx* ... ; it is to be seen in the *sarx* and nowhere else.'[12]

When one takes exception to this and observes, however, that this statement cannot mean that the Word became flesh and thus ceased to be the Word (who earlier was said to be in the beginning with God and who was God [1:1]), both because the Word is still the subject of the phrase that follows, 'and dwelt among us,' and because John's sequel to this latter phrase is 'and we beheld his glory *as* [the *hos* here denotes not only

---

9.   Rudolph Bultmann, *The Gospel of John*, Oxford, 1971, p. 61.
10.   *Ibid.*
11.   *Ibid.*, p. 62; *cf.* too his statement: 'It is in his sheer humanity that he is the Revealer', p. 63.
12.   *Ibid.*, pp. 62f., 69.

comparison but also identification] of the unique Son of the
Father, 'whom John then further describes as 'the unique one,
God himself, [cf. F. F. Bruce], who is in the bosom of the
Father' (1:18), one has just reason to wonder at the exegesis
behind Bultmann's response that John's assertions are reflecting
the perspective of *faith* which has understood that the revelation
of *God* is located precisely in the *humanity* of Jesus,[13]and that
they are not statements about the divine *being* of Jesus but rather
the mythological shaping of the *meaning* of Jesus for faith!

Can the exegete who is not a follower of the highly personal,
individualistic, existential school of Bultmann be blamed if he
politely demurs at this perspective? For here there remains not
even a kenotic Christ who once was God and who divested
himself of his deity but only an existential Christ who in *being*
never was or is God but who is only the Revealer of God to
faith, butof course this faith here is devoid of any historical
facticity.

The questions must be squarely faced: Is Bultmann's
interpretation preferable to that of Chalcedon? Is it in any sense
exegetically sustainable? Is not the language of John 1:14 the
language of an *eyewitness* (cf. the following 'we beheld' and
the commentary on this phrase in 1 John 1:1-3)? And does not
the Evangelist declare that others (cf. the 'we') as well as he
'beheld his glory,' which glory he identifies as *(hos)* the glory
of his divine being as 'unique Son of the Father'? And just
how observable Jesus' divine glory is is evident on every page,
in every sign-miracle he performed, a glory which neither
bystander could overlook nor enemy deny (cf. 2:11; 3:2; 9:16;
11:45-48; 12:10-12, 37-41; cf. Acts 2:22: 'as you yourselves
know'; cf., too, Acts 4:16: ' ... and we cannot deny it').[14]

---

13. *Ibid.*, pp. 62f., 69.
14. It is directly germane to our point here to observe in connection
with Christ's first sign miracle (John 2:1-11) that John does not
say that the disciples' faith was the pathway to the beholding of
Jesus' glory, but to the contrary, that his miracle manifested his
glory, and his disciples believed on him *as a consequence.*

Later, when doubting Thomas eventually comes to faith in Jesus and cries out, 'My Lord and my God' (20:28), he does so not because an existential flash bringing new pistic appreciation of the meaning of the human Jesus for human existence overpowered him, but because his demand to see the print of the nails with his own eyes was graciously met (cf. John 20:25, 27, 29), and because the only possible implication of Christ's resurrection appearance for the nature of his *being* (cf. Rom.1:4) made its inescapable impact upon him: 'He is my Lord and my God!'

Bultmann's Christology, only one of many examples of a Christology 'from below.' represents one extreme to which faulty theologizing can lead the church - the extreme of portraying the Christ as to his being as a mere man and only a man. But this conclusion not only the Fourth Gospel but also the New Testament as a whole finds intolerable. A careful consideration of each context will show that Jesus has the Greek word for 'God' *(theos)* ascribed to him at least eight times in the New Testament (John 1:1,18; 20:28; 1 John 5:20; Rom. 9:5; Tit. 2:13; Heb. 1:8; 2 Pet. 1:1; cf. also Col. 2:9). Hundreds of times he is called *kurios,* 'Lord,' the Greek word employed by the LXX to translate the Hebrew Tetragrammaton (cf., for example, Matt. 7:21; 25:37,44; Rom. 10:9-13; 1 Cor. 2:8; 12:3; 2 Cor. 4:5; Phil. 2:11; 2 Thes. 1:7-10). Old Testament statements spoken by or describing Yahweh, the Old Testament God of the covenant, are applied to Christ in the New (cf., for example, Ps. 102:25-27 and Heb. 1:10-12; Isa. 6:1-10 and John 12:40-41; Isa. 8:12-13 and 1 Pet. 3:14-15; Isa. 45:22 and Matt .11:28; Joel 2:32 and Rom. 10:13). Divine attributes and actions are ascribed to him (Mark 2:5, 8; Matt.18:20; John 8:58; Matt. 24:30). Then there is Jesus' own self-consciousness of his divine nature (cf. John 3:13; 6:38,46,62; 8:23,42; 17:6,24; and the famous so-called 'embryonic Fourth Gospel' in Matt.11:25-28 and Luke 10:21-22). Finally, the weight of testimony which flows from his miracles and his resurrection (Rom. 1:4) must be faced without evasion. It carries one beyond the bounds of credulity to be asked to believe that the several New Testament writers, living and writing under such varying circumstances, places, and times, were nonetheless all seduced by the same mythology of Gnosticism. All the more is this conclusion highly doubtful in light of the fact that the very presence of a pre-Christian Gnosticism has been seriously challenged by much recent scholarship.[15]

Käsemann's Docetic Christ

Now, very interestingly, it is by one of Bultmann's students, Ernst Käsemann, that we find argued the other extreme in current Christology.[16] In his *The Testimony of Jesus,* Käsemann also deals at some length with the meaning of John 1:14. He argues that the Evangelist intends by *sarx* here 'not the means to veil the glory of God in the man Jesus, but just the opposite, to reveal that glory before every eye. The flesh is the medium of the glory.'[17]

According to Käsemann, John's Jesus, far from being a man, is rather the portrayal of a god walking across the face of the earth. Commenting on 'the Word became flesh,' Käsemann queries: 'Is not this statement totally over-shadowed by the confession, "We behold his glory," so that it receives its meaning from

---

15. *Cf.* Edwin M. Yamauchi, *Pre-Christian Gnosticism: A Survey of the Proposed Evidence,* Grand Rapids, 1983, particularly Chapter 12; *cf.* also C.H. Dodd, *The Interpretation of the Fourth Gospel* (1953); the Dodd *Festschrift, The Background of the New Testament and Its Eschatology,* especially the articles by W.F. Albright and R.P. Casey; and R.E. Brown, *The Gospel According to John I-XII,* p. LVI.

16. I am indebted to Herman N. Ridderbos for calling my attention to this contrast between teacher and student. *Cf.* 'The Word Became Flesh,' *Through Christ's Word* (Phillipsburg, New Jersey, 1985), pp. 3-22, especially p. 5.

17. Ridderbos, *op.cit.,* p. 6.

it?'[18]   Thinking it to be so, Käsemann contends that the Fourth Gospel uses the earthly life of Jesus 'merely as a backdrop for the Son of God proceeding through the world ...'[19] Furthermore, he urges: ' ... the glory of Jesus determines [the Evangelist's] whole presentation so thoroughly from the very outset that the incorporation and position of the passion narrative of necessity becomes problematical,'[20] so problematical, in fact, Käsemann believes, that 'one is tempted to regard it as being a mere postscript [*nachklappt*] which had to be included because John could not ignore this tradition nor yet could he fit it organically into his work.'[21]   So great is John's emphasis on the divine glory of Jesus that, according to Käsemann, the Fourth Gospel has slipped into a 'naïve docetism':

> John [formulated who Jesus was and is] in his own manner. In so doing he exposed himself to dangers ... One can hardly fail to recognize the danger of his Christology of glory, namely, the danger of docetism. It is present in a still naïve, unreflected form ...[22]

In sum, John 'was able to give an answer [to the question of the centre of the Christian message] only in the form of a naïve docetism,'[23] Jesus' humanity really playing no role as it stands 'entirely in the shadow' of Jesus' glory as 'something quite non-essential.'[24]   'In what sense', Käsemann asks, 'is he flesh, who walks on the water and through closed doors, who cannot be captured by his enemies, who at the well of Samaria

---

18. *The Testament of Jesus: A Study of the Gospel of John In the Light of Chapter 1*, Philadelphia, 1968, pp. 9-10.
19. *Ibid.*, p. 13.
20. *Ibid.*, p. 7.
21. *Ibid.*
22. *Ibid.*, pp. 26, 77; *cf.* his statement: 'The assertion, quite generally accepted today, that the Fourth Gospel is anti-docetic is completely unproven' (p. 26, n. 41).
23. *Ibid.*, p. 26.
24. Ridderbos, *op.cit.*, p. 9.

is tired and desires a drink, yet has no need of drink and has
food different from that which his disciples seek? ... How
does all this agree with the understanding of a realistic
incarnation?'[25] he seriously doubts whether 'the "true man" of
later incarnational theology becomes believable' in John's
Christology.[26]

What is one to say about Käsemann's opposite extreme to that
of Bultmann? One can only applaud the emphasis here on the
'very God' character of Jesus, but surely Ridderbos is right
when, commenting on John 1:14, he writes:

> Egeneto, 'became,' is not there for nothing. It is surely
> a matter of a new mode of existence. Also, not
> accidental is the presence of sarx, 'flesh,' which ...
> indicates man in his weakness, vulnerability, and
> transiency. Therefore, it has been said, not incorrectly,
> that this statement ... certainly approximates the opposite
> of what one would expect if it were spoken of a docetic
> ... world of thought.[27]

Moreover, nowhere is Jesus' humanity more apparent in a
natural and unforced way than in John's Gospel. Our Lord can
grow weary from a journey, sit down at a well for a moment of
respite, and ask for water. He calls himself (8:40) and is called
by others a man (anthropos) many times (4:29; 5:12; 7:46;
9:11; 16, 24; 10:33; 11:47; 18:17,29; 19:5). People know
his father and mother (6:42; 7:27; 1:45). He can spit on the

25. Käsemann, op.cit.,p. 9.
26. Ibid., p. 10.
27. Ridderbos, op.cit., p.10. The reference in the last sentence is to
the opinions of R. Schnackenburg, Das Johannesevanglium, p.
244, and R.E. Brown, The Gospel According to John, p. 24.
But one could add almost indefinitely to this list the names of
scholars who view John as self-consciously opposing docetism
by his statement in 1:14, for example, Leon Morris, The Gospel
According to John Grand Rapids, 1971, p. 102, and F.F. Bruce,
The Gospel of John Grand Rapids, 1983, pp. 39-40.

ground and make mud with his saliva (9:6). He can weep over the sorrow Lazarus' death brings to Mary and Martha (11:35). He can be troubled (*he psuche mou tetaraktai*) as he contemplates his impending death on the cross (12:27). Here is clearly a *man,* for whom death was no friend, who could instinctively recoil against it as a powerful enemy to be feared and resisted. He can have a crown of thorns pressed down on his head (19:2) and be struck in the face (19:3). At his crucifixion (N.B.!) a special point[28] is made of the spear thrust in his side (cf. *soma,* 19:38, 40), from which wound blood and water flowed forth (19:34). And after his resurrection on at least two occasions he shows his disciples his hands and feet, and even eats breakfast with them by the Sea of Galilee. Here is no docetic Christ! Clearly, in John's Christology we have to do with *sarx,* 'flesh,' a man in weakness and vulnerability, a 'true man.' In Käsemann's interpretation of John's Jesus, while we certainly have to do with a Christology 'from above,' the Christ therein is so 'wholly other' that his humanity is only a 'costume' and no part of a genuine incarnation.

Where precisely does the biblical material in John lead us, however (and here I turn to my own theologizing)? Does not a fair reading of John's testimony in its entirety yield up a Jesus who is true man, and yet at the same time One who is more (not other) than true man? And in what direction are we instructed to look for the meaning of this 'more than' save the 'more than' of the Son of God who is just the One who was with God the Father in the beginning and who himself was and is God (John 1:1-3), who 'for us men and for our salvation,' without ceasing to be what he is, took into union with himself what he was not and became a man, and as the God-man entered the world through the virgin's womb?

---

28. *Cf.* John 19:35: 'The man who saw it has given testimony, and his teaching is true.'

And what about Käsemann's suggestion that the Fourth Gospel's *theologia gloriae* so overpowers everything in its path that there is really no room in it for a *theologia crucis,* that John brings it in simply because he cannot ignore the tradition?   I respectfully submit that such a perspective emanates from his own theological system rather than from exegesis and objective analysis.   The *theologia crucis* fits as comfortably in John's Gospel as it does in the Synoptics or elsewhere.   It is introduced at the outset in the Forerunner's 'Behold the Lamb' (1:26,29) and continues throughout as an integral aspect of John's Christology, for example, in the several references to the 'hour' that was to come upon Jesus (2:4; 7:30; 8:20; 12:23; 13:1;   17:1), in Jesus' Good Shepherd discourse where he reveals that he would lay down his life for the sheep (10:11,15), and in his teaching of the grain of seed which must die (12:24).

It must be clearly seen that the implication in Käsemann's intimation that the dogma of a *divine* Saviour does violence to a theology of the *cross* would mortally wound Christianity as the redemptive religion of God at its very heart, for both Christ's deity and Christ's cross are essential to our salvation.   But the implication of Käsemann's point is just to the opposite effect: that one can have a theology of glory or a theology of the cross, but one cannot have both simultaneously.   But, I ask, do not these two stand as friends side by side throughout the New Testament?   Paul, for example, whose theology is specifically a theology of the cross can, even as John, see precisely *in the cross* Christ's glory and triumph over the kingdom of darkness (Col. 2:15).   The writer of Hebrews can affirm that it is precisely *by his death* that Jesus destroyed the devil and liberated those enslaved by the fear of death (2:14-15). Clearly, Käsemann's construction cannot be permitted to stand unchallenged for it plays one scriptural theme off over against a second equally scriptural theme which in no way is intrinsically contradictory to it.

Is there a sense, then, in the light of all of this, in which we may legitimately speak of both kinds of Christologies - 'from above' and 'from below' - in the Gospels? I believe there is, but in the sense clarified by the great Princeton theologian, Benjamin B. Warfield, now over seventy-five years ago:

> John's Gospel does not differ from the other Gospels as the Gospel of the divine Christ in contradistinction to the Gospels of the human Christ. All the Gospels are Gospels of the divine Christ ... But John's Gospel differs from the other Gospels in taking from the divine Christ its starting point. The others begin on the plane of human life. John begins in the inter-relations of the divine persons in eternity.

> [The Synoptic Gospels] all begin with the man Jesus, whom they set forth as the Messiah in whom God has visited his people; or rather, as himself, God come to his people, according to his promise. The movement in them is from below upward ... The movement in John, on the contrary, is from above downward. he takes his start from the Divine Word, and descends from him to the human Jesus in whom he was incarnated. This Jesus, say the others, is God. This God, says John, became Jesus.[29]

By these last paragraphs I have illustrated what I think the theological task is and how it is to be fulfilled. Our task as theologians is simply to listen to and to seek to understand and to explicate what we hear in the Holy Scriptures in their entirety for the health and benefit of the church and in order to enhance the faithful propagation of the true gospel. With a humble spirit and the best use of grammatical/historical tools of exegesis we should draw out of Scripture, always being sensitive to all of its well-balanced nuances, the truth of God revealed therein. If we are to emulate our Lord, his apostles, and the New Testament church, that and that alone is our task. As we do so, we are to

---

29. Benjamin B. Warfield, 'John's First Word,' *Selected Shorter Writings of Benjamin B. Warfield*, edited by John E. Meeter; Nutley, New Jersey, 1970, vol. I, pp. 148-149.

wage a tireless war against any and every effort of the many hostile existentialist and humanist philosophies which abound about us to influence the results of our labours.

Have we solved all of the problems inherent in the church dogma of a two-natured Christ by this method? In my opinion we have not. Further inquiry is needed for example, into the doctrine of the eternal generation of the Son,[30] into the doctrine of the *anhypostasia*, and how, for example, the *same* person simultaneously can be ignorant of some things (Mark 13:32; Luke 2:52) and yet know all things (Matt.9:4; John 1:47; 2:25; 11:11, 14). But the fact that problems remain for him as he carries out the task incumbent upon him gives the theologian no warrant to play one Scripture truth off against another (for example, Christ's deity over against his humanity, or a theology of glory over against a theology of the cross) and to reject one clear emphasis in Scripture out of deference for another of equal prominence which he may happen to prefer. And it is right here - in his willingness to submit his mind to all of Scripture - *pasa graphe* (2 Tim.3:16) - that the theologian as a student of the Word most emulates the example of his Lord (cf. Matt.4:4, 7, 10; 5:17-18; Luke 24:27 [notice the reference to 'all the Scriptures']; John 10:35). And it is in such submission to Scripture that the theologian best reflects that disciple character to which he has by grace been called as he goes about his task.

---

30. It is encouraging to see in the writings of such men as John Calvin, Charles Hodge, Benjamin Warfield, John Murray, J. Oliver Buswell, and Donald Macleod the Nicene Creed's implicit subordination of the Son to the Father, in modes of subsistence as well as in operation, being called into question and corrected.

THE HOLY SPIRIT AND HERMENEUTICS

JAN VEENHOF

In this contribution we will deal with the significance of the Holy Spirit for hermeneutics, namely the hermeneutics of Holy Scripture. We are confronted immediately with various questions which come to the fore in discussions about hermeneutics; discussions which occur within theology, but primarily within philosophy, literature and linguistic sciences. I would like to remind you briefly of some aspects of these discussions, which are important for our subject.

In accordance with the original meaning of the Greek root, 'hermeneutics' indicates the theory of explanation and interpretation of texts. To this belongs the knowledge of the language of the text and its grammar, feeling for the individual use of language of an author, attention to the scope of a text and to the context of the text, and so on. This meaning remained dominant until the nineteenth century. In this sense the term was also used within theology as an indication of a special discipline, dealing with the exegesis of the Bible. Often the distinction was made between this theological hermeneutics as *hermeneutica sacra* and hermeneutics in a general sense, *hermeneutica profana*. Later I will return to this distinction.[1]

In the nineteenth century a change comes in the picture, which continues in our century. This change caused a great expansion of the content of the term. Under the influence of men such as Schleiermacher and Dilthey an intensive reflection began on questions which previously only implicitly came into discussion. All these questions revolve around the idea of understanding. What is the essence of it? Under which

---

1. *Cf.* for this distinction S. Greijdanus, *Schriftbeginselen ter Schriftverklaring,* Kampen, 1946, pp. 11f. The New Testament scholar Greijdanus (1871-1948) who was a pupil of Kuyper and Bavinck and taught in Kampen for many years defends here the justness of a specific *hermeneutica sacra.*

Jan Veenhof

conditions is understanding realised? Which historical changes are evident in these conditions? These are the questions, which in recent times – I mention here only the name of Gadamer – are analysed intensively. This does not imply that the old conception of the task of hermeneutics has been completely put aside. But it has been integrated now in a broader context, in which exegesis and understanding are discussed together. This connection seems justified. As we will see in the following, there is a continuous interaction between them, although it is not correct to equate them.[2]

Exegesis and understanding – they certainly influence each other. To perceive this it is only necessary to realise what is

---

2. The literature about hermeneutics is overwhelmingly extensive. I must restrict myself to the mention of the following publications which offer a general and fundamental orientation: J.M. Robinson and J.B. Cobb, *New Frontiers in Theology,* I *The Later Heidegger and Theology,* II *New Hermeneutics,* III *Theology as History,* New York-Evanston-London, 1963-1967; F. Mussner, *Geschichte der Hermeneutik von Schleiermacher bis zur Gegenwart,* in M. Schmaus a.o. (editors) *Handbuch der Dogmengeschichte,* Band I Faszikel 3c (2.Teil), Freiburg-Basle-Wien, 1970; H. Cazelles, *Écriture, Parole et Esprit. Trois Aspects de l'Hermeneutique Biblique,* Paris, 1971; E. Hufnagle *Einführung in die Hermeneutik,* Urban Taschenbücher 233, Stuttgart-Berlin-Köln-Mainz, 1976; L.D. Derksen, *On Universal Hermeneutics. A Study in the Philosophy of Hans-Georg Gadamer,* (Dissertation, Free University, Amsterdam), Amsterdam, 1983; G. Scholtz, *Die Philosophie Schleiermachers,* Darmstadt, 1984. Other publications are mentioned in the following footnotes. As for the relation between interpretation and understanding I should like to point here to the fact that a man like O.A. Dilschneider stresses the difference against tendencies to level both, *cf.* his *Ich Glaube an den Heiligen Geist. Versuch einer Kritik und Antwort zur Existenztheologie,* Wuppertal, 1969, pp. 46-51. Whatever may be said about the relation, the fundamental nature of understanding in my opinion cannot be questioned. Interpretation finds its origin in understanding and intends to lead to understanding.

106

inherent in the idea of understanding. Profiting from the insights, developed by Gadamer and others, in Dutch Reformed circles H.M. Vroom has clarified this in his writings. I should like to draw attention to several elements of his exposition. For the understanding of what another says it is necessary that I am involved in the matter about which the other speaks, and I must have an idea of the context, the situation, in which the other says what he does. Furthermore, there are important questions either sociological or psychological, which can enable us to understand – or can block understanding. Especially important are the values which are accepted. They form an essential part of the frame of reference within which we understand. This frame of reference is of decisive significance for the question whether and how we take in and employ new information. We can summarise all these factors with the term 'horizon of understanding'. This is a technical term, which indicates all that we have brought with us as our cultural, mental and spiritual baggage.[3]

All this is true in a specific way for the understanding of written texts, including texts of the past, of which the Bible is one; but especially when these texts not only afford objective information but touch elementary questions of life. The writers of the Bible had another horizon of understanding, they lived in another world from ours. And it is necessary that we be conscious of it, because otherwise we read our own insights into the Bible – especially in the area of religion.[4]

---

3.   H.M. Vroom, *Naar letter en geest. Over het beroep op de Bijbel*, Kampen, 1981, pp. 93-97. This publication affords the elaboration of a number of insights, which he defended with an expanded scientific documentation in his book, *De Schrift alleen? Een vergelijkend onderzoek naar de toetsing van theologische uitspraken volgens de openbaringstheologische visie van Torrance en de hermeneutisch-theologische opvattingen van Van Buren, Ebeling, Moltmann en Pannenberg*, (Dissertation, Free University, Amsterdam), Kampen, 1978. *Cf.* for the viewpoints recorded by me especially pp. 221-231.
4.   *Naar letter en geest*, pp. 97-102.

That is one side of the matter: our horizon of understanding, if we are not conscious of it, can block or restrict the understanding. But there is also another side. Our horizon of understanding plays also an indispensable role in a positive sense in the understanding of texts. We understand a text only as we bring into play our own life-experience, if we actualise the content of the stories in connection with our own situation.[5]

It is the task of the professional historical critical interpretation to clarify the horizon of understanding of the writers of the text of the past. This interpretation serves the understanding but is not this understanding itself. The real understanding lies in what Gadamer indicates as the coalescence of both horizons. The text and our own time and world come together. 'The penny drops'. 'It clicks'. 'It catches fire'. We see and hear in the text something that touches us. To say it better: the text becomes a word which grasps us. So the story of the text becomes an impulse in the formation of our life-story.[6]

So far these considerations of Vroom. We can deduce from them that present hermeneutics indeed deals with the whole process of understanding. Now you could ask the question, why this was not explicitly discussed earlier. The reason may be that the horizon of the understanding of the reality and of the human self-experience since the time in which the text came into existence, had not undergone great changes. Of course there were already changes, and of course there was the act of translation necessary, which is according to the root of the verb the bringing of something from the one area to another. But these changes took place slowly; so slowly that often they were unconscious.

The fundamental problem of understanding was felt only after the rapid change of the horizon in later times, as a consequence

---

5. *Naar letter en geest*, pp. 102-104.
6. *Naar letter en geest*, pp. 104-108.

of which the questions of a text from the past, and still stronger the notions and images which stamped the answers in the text, were felt as strange. In that case the question arises: what has that to do with our life? When we reflect about it the question arises: under what conditions is it possible for people of different times to understand each other, especially in that which touches their essential existence? This situation, in which we observe the accelerated changes in life and in the experience of reality, has arisen in the last two centuries; and in the twentieth century it is more manifest than ever before. From this we can explain the rise of the new hermeneutics.[7]

In the light of the new hermeneutics we can describe the whole process of interpretation and understanding as a connection of different but interdependent elements.[8]   I can summarise now the most important ones.

1.*The so-called 'previous understanding' (Vorverständnis)*, the consciousness (perhaps vague) of the matter dealt with in the text. The interpreter brings such a consciousness with him and presupposes it also in those for whom he interprets and who have to receive the possibility of genuine understanding. This consciousness is not sacrosanct, unassailable.   In the task of interpretation and understanding it has to be risked, at any rate tested.   Were it not so, the text would not be able to say anything new, anything relevant. In that case the interpretation (*sc.,* the understanding) would only confirm the opinions we have already and would be senseless. So the question is how we can prevent that previous understanding from dominating in such a manner that our interpretation – including our understanding from the very beginning – is stamped by our own prior convictions and preoccupations? In this connection one often speaks about a hermeneutical circle. It would be better to speak of a hermeneutical spiral.   'Circle' implies that the

---

7.   These insights are a dominant factor in the structure and elaboration of the Christological concept of E. Schillebeeckx.
8.   *Cf.* the surveys in the publications of Mussner and Cazelles mentioned in n2.

previous understanding in the process of understanding, as it were, returns to itself. But that is – happily – not an absolute necessity. The understanding of a text can also do something with the interpreter, reader, hearer; can transform them.[9]

2. *A leading interest.* All interpretation takes place from a certain interest, with a certain intention and expectation. This interest is one of the determining factors of the question which is directed to a text. The interest of the interpreter, reader, hearer meets the interest of the text, so that the question of the relation between both interests becomes actual.[10]

3. *The historical reconstruction.* This reconstruction intends to make a picture of the horizon in which the texts come into existence. This takes place by means of historical analysis. Here the technical rules of hermeneutics come into play. Such historical analysis is not easy. Complete objectivity is, with the exception of certain details, unattainable, because the researcher always brings with him his own horizon of understanding. But nevertheless openness is possible which does not interpret away what is strange – whether in an historical, ethical or religious sense.[11]

9.	*Cf.* for the idea of *Vorverständnis e.g.* O. Weber, *Grundlagen der Dogmatik*, I, Neukirchen, 1955, 144. Weber points to the fact that since Dilthey the relationship between the author and the interpreter is acknowledged as a presupposition of the understanding. Formerly the term 'congeniality' (*cf.* n34) was used as indication of that presupposition. The philosophy of existence placed instead of the term 'congeniality' that of *Vorverständnis* in the centre.
10.	This viewpoint is a dominant aspect of the Latin-American theology of liberation, *cf., e.g* ., J. Sobrino, *Christology at the Crossroads. A Latin American Approach*, London, 1981.
11.	*Cf.* the well-documented expositions of Colin Brown in his contribution 'History and the Believer', in Colin Brown, ed., *History, Criticism and Faith*, Leicester, 1976, pp. 147-216.

4. *The discovery of scope.* The scope is the central idea or intention of a greater or smaller unit of text. Interpretation is not reproduction of a conglomerate of statements, but the approach to a coherent understanding from the centre which this idea supplies. With 'scope' is not meant an arbitrary perspective, but the fundamental point of view of the texts themselves.[12]

5. *Translating into the horizon of the present.* Only when a text is interpreted and understood is it possible to relate its statements, especially its scope, to the viewpoints and questions of the interpreter's own horizon of experiences.[13]

We return now to theology, and ask how the hermeneutical problem presents itself within theological reflection. Older theology distinguished, as I have already indicated, between *hermeneutica sacra* and *profana.* This distinction recognises, in the first place, that the object of the *hermeneutica sacra* is different principally from all other writings because of its divine origin and character. In the second place this distinction recognises that for interpretation according to the rules of this *hermeneutica sacra* the assistance of the Holy Spirit is absolutely necessary.[14] This conviction lived within post-Reformation Protestant orthodoxy. Orthodox theology wished to establish, with its strict doctrine of inspiration, the divine origin and character of Scripture: the Bible is in every respect the book of the Spirit. Orthodoxy taught that the 'objective' historical knowledge of Scripture already requires the assistance of the Spirit, although this knowledge is not yet connected with *fiducia*

---

12. *Cf.* for the idea of 'scope' G.C. Berkouwer, *De Heilige Schrift I,* Kampen, 1966, pp. 175-180 and *De Heilige Schrift II* , Kampen, 1967, pp. 95-100.
13. *Cf.* H. Ott in his contribution 'Hermeneutik als Fundament der Pneumatologie', in O.A. Dilschneider, ed., *Theologie des Geistes,* Gütersloh, 1980, pp. 97-107.
14. W. Schmithals, 'Wissenschaftliches Verstehen und Existentielles Verstehen im Geiste', in Dischneider, ed., *Theologie des Geistes,* p. 114 (see note 13).

(confidence).   Scientific exegesis has to be 'pneumatic'
exegesis.[15]   Early 'classical' Pietism laid less stress on the
connection of the Spirit with the book.   Rather it accentuated in
a new way the connection of the Spirit with the interpreter,
reader and hearer of the book: the personally experienced
operation of the Holy Spirit is a precondition for the
understanding of Scripture.   The similarity with Orthodoxy lies
in the conviction that no understanding of the Bible is possible
without the Holy Spirit.   But according to Pietism – and here
lies the difference – the Holy Spirit is not primarily connected
with the Word but with the understanding man.   Only a reborn
Christian is able to understand the Scripture truly.[16]

An essential change was brought about by the arrival of
historical critical investigation on the scene of theology.   The
first representatives of historical criticism – I think of men like
Eichhorn and Semler – were of the opinion that the distinction
of *hermeneutica sacra* and *profana* could no longer hold.
Insofar as the Bible is an historical book, it has to be interpreted
in an historical manner as much as other historical writings,
without any dogmatic preoccupation.   And for this the Holy
Spirit is not necessary.   This does not mean that these men
deny the operation of the Holy Spirit, but they give it another
role.   So Semler distinguishes the scientific understanding and
the work of the Holy Spirit as the natural true correct
understanding and the supernatural living understanding.   The

15. Schmithals, *op. cit.* p. 114.   See for the doctrine of Scripture in the
     Post-Reformation theology my *Revelatie en Inspiritie.   De
     Openbarings - en Schriftbeschouwing van Herman Bavinck in
     vergelijking met die der ethische theologie*, Amsterdam, 1967, pp. 13-
     28.
16. Schmithals, *op. cit.*, p. 114, *cf.* G. Maier, *Heiliger Geist und
     Schriftauslegung*, Wuppertal, 1983, p. 10: in the period of Pietism
     'rückt die Person des Auslegers in den Mittelpunkt des Interesses, in
     dem die theologia regenitorum betont wird'.   The accent was thus
     shifted – to a certain extent – from the inspired Scripture to the
     inspired interpreter.

illumination of the Holy Spirit affects only the living understanding.[17]

This view became increasingly the dominating one in theology. The old distinction, which I mentioned before, was pushed into the background. The opinion became predominant that there is only one hermeneutics. For the interpretation of the Bible the same principles and methods are valid as for all interpretation of texts from the past. Often the distinction was made – in manifold variation of the distinction of Semler – between a historical objective and an existential subjective or personal understanding. The former is a matter of methodological reflection, accessible in principle to everyone. It is certainly not a purely intellectual understanding. It may be a congenial understanding, which observes the appeal in the text. Another question however is, how someone reacts on this appeal. This is no longer a matter of methodological reflection, but the expression of a personal engagement. Such an engagement is characteristic for the personal understanding.[18]

It is difficult to select here the right terms, because the impact of those terms depends on the content which is given to them. Authors use many varying descriptions. But in some way or another they speak of two 'phases', two 'dimensions', or whatever qualification may be given. Some authors distinguish even more than two phases or dimensions. What is common to all of them is the conviction that such a differentiation is possible, justified and indeed obligatory.[19] Personally I plead for the correctness of such differentiation, which is – and I like to stress that! – different from a separation. It seems to me that the formal structure of the hermeneutical process within

---

17. Schmithals, *op. cit.*, pp. 115f.
18. *Cf.* G. Maier, *Wie legen wir die Schrift aus?*, Geissen und Basel, 1978.
19. *Cf. e.g.*, J. Barr, *Explorations in Theology, 7. The Scope and Authority of the Bible,* London, 1978.

theology is the same as elsewhere.[20] The elements I mentioned before confirm this. To this extent there is no specific Biblical hermeneutics. At the same time there is in the hermeneutical theological approach to the Bible something specific. The expectation with which, within theology, interpretation deals with the texts is of a specific nature. This expectation is : *via* human statements of and in the texts the voice, the calling of God will grasp us. This expectation is confirmed by the experience of the church in its 'conversation' with the Bible. The deepest foundation of this expectation is the promise, testified in the Bible, that in the word of the witnesses the Lord himself will be present. I am conscious of the fact that this implies an *a priori* of faith. And I do not hesitate to say that openly, seeing that no one is without an *a priori*.[21] Through this expectation the interpretation within theology gets its own direction. It is the aim to interpret the texts in such a manner that the Word, which brought forth these texts, is conserved in its continuous identity and at the same time in its steadily actual relevance. The Word is the Word of God, who comes to men in Jesus. This implies the permanent identity of the Word, for Jesus Christ is the permanent ground, content and norm of faith. No interpretation can be the true one which detracts from that permanent identity. This permanent identity however does not mean that the Word is bound to or even imprisoned in a past period, or restricted to a past culture. Jesus is the same, yesterday, now and in eternity (Heb. 13:8). That means that he in all the phases of history is who he was during his stay on earth; the One who is surprisingly new. Jesus is never antiquated. He is permanently actual and relevant. And the same is true of his Word. In close connection with the changing situations in which men find

---

20. In this opinion I am confirmed by the observation of the fact that defenders of a specific biblical hermeneutic nevertheless make several reservations, cf., Greijdanus *op. cit.*, p. 12 and Maier, *Heiliger Geist und Schriftauslegung*, pp. 36ff.
21. I will mark off with emphasis this *a priori* in the sense of a previous judgment that contains a preoccupation which blocks the way to understanding.

themselves, it speaks in a new way to us. We may say it also like this: in close connection with these changing situations we discover new things in that word.[22] As for this discovery, it must be taken into account that God's revealing of his saving truth and our discovery of it are not two separated phenomena. God will reveal himself in the way of our seeking and finding, in which process God has the permanent initiative. It is said rightly: 'In the insights which men find a creative process of seeking – these insights are concrete truths – the staying Truth of God comes to us.'[23]

The secret of this comprehensive event is the work of the Holy Spirit, who on the basis of the revelation in Christ will guide the disciples into all truth (John 16:13). The Spirit is the One who bridges the distance between the past and the present and lets us see and meet Jesus, the Son of God, sent by the Father; and in Jesus the Father himself. That is the greatness of the work of the Spirit, that in all reflection about hermeneutical questions in connection with the Bible comes to us as a surprising and overwhelming reality.[24] Now it is important to keep in mind the nature of this work. I kept a distance before from speaking about a *hermeneutica sacra*. In the conception of such a hermeneutics the endeavour manifests itself to mark off the acting of God in and through men, as it were 'quantitatively', from all that is being done in, with, and by men. A similar endeavour can be observed among those who at any cost will 'fix' the specific nature of Christian ethics 'substantially', 'materially', in virtues and deeds which can be found only in

---

22. *Cf.* my *De parakleet. Enige beschouwingen over de parakleet-belofte in het evangelie van Johannes en haar theologische betekenis*, Kampen, 1977, pp. 22-25.
23. J.G. Schaap, *Samen leren leven en geloven. Een godsdienstpaedagogisch onderzoek naar het omgaan met kernwoorden van geloven in situaties van dialogisch leren en begeleiden* (Dissertation, Free University, Amsterdam), Gravenhage, 1984, p. 171.
24. *Cf.* my *De parakleet*, p. 32.

Christians.[25]   Or also among those who, at any cost, will maintain the 'supernatural' character of the New Testament *charismata*, to mark them materially off from all so-called 'natural' gifts.[26]

But none of these efforts succeeds.   It becomes clear that the work of the Spirit cannot be described in terms of 'addition', as if the Spirit would give or cause a new 'quantum', a new 'substance'.   On the contrary the work of the Spirit must be described in terms of relation and interaction.[27]   According to this view man is brought by the Spirit to a new situation, characterised by his relation to God.   This view is confirmed by what the Biblical testimony says about the work of the Spirit. From very different points of view and in very different ways it comes to expression, that the Spirit brings about our relation to God in Christ.   It is by the Spirit that we can know God in Christ, and so can come into relation to him.[28]   I confine myself here to the explicit reference in the passage 1 Cor. 2:10-16, which is of fundamental importance for our subject.   In this massive passage, packed full with thoughts about the Spirit, Paul stresses the facts that all that is mediated by the Spirit – the whole revelation of God in Christ – can be discerned and accepted in its true nature only by spiritual, 'pneumatical', people.   Dilschneider points rightly to the fact that the central moment in this passage is the '*homoion*-thesis', which has been proposed from ancient times until now: the equal can only be

---

25.   *Cf.* for the discussions about a *proprium* of Christian ethics, D.E. de Villiers, *Die eiesoortigheid van die Christelike moraal* (Dissertation, Free University, Amsterdam), Amsterdam, 1978.
26.   *Cf.* my contribution 'Charismata – bovennatuurlijk of natuurlijk?', in J.H. van de Bank e.a., edd., *Ervaren waarheid. Bundel voor H. Jonker,* Nijkerk, 1984, pp. 120-133.
27.   See my contribution mentioned in note 24, p. 130; also J. Firet in his article 'Psychologische notities met betrekking tot de Geestesdoop', in *Gereformeerd Theologisch Tijdschrift* 78 (1978), pp. 87f.
28.   *Cf. my article* 'Pontifex Maximus' in *Gereformeerd Theologisch Tijdschrift* 78 (1978) pp. 4-15.

known and understood by the equal, *simile simili cognosci*. This thesis is formulated by Paul in its positive but also in its negative fashion. The pneumatical must be discerned, perceived pneumatically; and at the same time, the physical man does not accept what comes from the Spirit of God.

This *homoion*-thesis brings us, according to Dilschneider, into a specific epistemological position. It makes clear that we have to see the understanding in respect of the knowing of faith. At any rate it is clear that here the Cartesian subject-object scheme is broken. For the object of that knowing – the things of the Spirit – is that which determines the knowing human subject. The man who knows by faith stands in the reality, in the field of operation of the Spirit, and is in his knowing fully dependent on that operation. This object remains always subject![29] In Scottish theology this viewpoint has been expressed by Thomas F. Torrance in an impressive way.[30] As it is the Spirit who

---

29. *Cf* Dilschneider, *Ich glaube an den Heiligen Geist*, pp. 51-54. See also Dischneider's contribution 'Gnoseologie oder vom Verstehen im Geiste' in *Theologie des Geistes* (see n13), pp. 59-68. The fact that God in the process of our knowing of him remains the Subject is testified with emphasis by such men as Kuyper, Bavinck and Barth.

30. Thomas F. Torrance says in his contribution 'The epistemological relevance of the Holy Spirit' in R. Schippers a.o. ed., *Ex auditu verbi. Bundel voor G.C. Berkouwer*, Kampen, 1965, pp. 282f, about our knowing of God as follows:

   'so that the given Object of our knowledge is actively at work in our knowing of it creating from our side a corresponding action in which our own being is committed. That is why theological thinking is essentially a spiritual activity in which we are engaged in a movement that corresponds to the movement of the Spirit and indeed participates in it. It is a form of kinetic thinking in which the reason does not apprehend the truth by sitting back and thinking ideas, but in an act or movement in which it participates in what it seeks to know. Thus in order to know Jesus Christ, the eternal Word become flesh, the Truth of God in historical happening, we must know Him

prays in us (Rom. 8:15), so it is also the Spirit who *knows* in us. Meanwhile we may say at the same time, without hesitation, that *we* are those who pray and who know. For when the Spirit grasps and fills a man he does not suppress that man, but he lets him or her function in full humanity. It is man who believes and knows, but ... through the Spirit of Christ. Man is no longer an autonomous subject. Certainly the man himself believes, but not out of, or from, himself.

We are here on the track of thoughts which had fundamental importance in the theology of the Reformers. Luther, for example, said the following: 'If there is a true faith it is a sure confidence of the heart and firm acknowledgement with which Christ is apprehended. So that Christ is the object of faith, rather however not object but to say it in this way, in faith Christ himself is present.'[31]

In the act of faith we are, as it were, taken out of our position as subjects. Therefore the *extra nos* is fundamental for this theology. Luther formulates it so: 'Therefore our whole theology is sure, because it places us outside of ourselves.'[32]

It is not the autonomous man who decides from out of himself to know and to understand. The knowing is here embedded in the being known. And this being known is mediated by the Spirit. Dilschneider rightly reminds us in this connection of the central function of the idea of the *testimonium Spiritus Sancti* in Luther and Calvin. The Spirit, under whose guidance the Bible

---

in a way apposite to that divine becoming and happening, in space and time, and therefore *kata pneuma*, as St. Paul said. This is what Kierkegaard used to call "the leap of faith", but it would be a grave misunderstanding to think of this as a blind or irrational movement, for it is the very reverse of that.'

31. See Luther, Weimarer Ausgabe 40, 1, pp. 228-229.
32. Luther, *Weimarer Ausgabe* 40, 1, p. 589. *Cf.* Dilschneider, *Ich glaube an den Heiligen Geist,* p. 56, where some more statements of Luther are quoted.

came into existence and by whose illumination men came to the true knowledge of the Scripture, is also the One who 'seals' the saving truth of the Gospel to the heart of the believer. By the Spirit believers are assured and convicted that in the Scripture God's saving truth comes to men, and in particular to themselves.[33] The Spirit opens Scripture for us and opens us for Scripture.

If we would have to summarise this insight in a succinct formula, we could try the following characterisation: by the Spirit, and only by the Spirit, we learn to hear and – in a certain measure – *see* God in Scripture, as he in Christ will be our, my God. That is the authentic understanding of Scripture, namely that understanding by means of which I understand myself newly in the light of God's saving intentions or, to say it in the terms of Calvin in the famous beginning of his *Institutes*, by means of which I came to the true knowledge of God and of myself. I should not like to qualify this as 'congeniality'. For congeniality implies in this case, that someone has an inner understanding, a 'feeling' for religious expressions and for the experiences which lie behind those expressions. Congeniality with a Psalmist implies that I can understand his experience of faith. This congeniality is a condition for the understanding, but it is not yet the understanding of the matter itself, or better, the Person himself.[34]

---

33. *Cf.* for the doctrine of the *testimonium Spiritus Sancti* of Calvin and later Reformed theologians my *Revelatie en Inspiratie* (see n15), pp. 489-499. See also G.P. Hartvelt, *Goed voor Gods Woord*, Kampen, 1969, pp. 54-57.

34. *Cf.*, for the idea of 'congeniality', note 9. This idea can be traced back to Dilthey but still further to the interpretation-traditions of Schleiermacher and Pietism. An advocate from more recent times is the New Testament scholar E. von Dobschütz. In his book *Vom Auslegen des Neuen Testaments*, Göttingen, 1926, p. 28, he formulated it in a vivid way. 'Wie ein Abstinent schwerlich der rechte Ausleger für die Lieder eines Anakreon oder der Sappho sein wird, so kann ein Mensch, der nicht gewisse Voraussetzungen mitbringt, sagen wir kurz, der nicht innerlich fromm ist, mag er noch

The one who understands genuinely is he who comes into a relation with the God about whom the Psalmist speaks. He or she recognises in what the Psalmist brings to expression his or her own experiences in the communion with God. He or she understands because he or she participates in the 'matter'. The interpreter who himself has a relationship with the God of the Psalmist asks, *via* the experiences and expressions of the Psalmist, of God himself.   Such an interpreter discovers for himself that it pleases God to reveal himself by means of the faith-experiences and faith-expressions of men.[35]

So the true understanding realises itself in the relation with God. This relation belongs from a methodological point of view to the 'previous understanding' *(Vorverständnis)* of the interpreter. And just here I should like to place the function of the Spirit in the process of interpreting and understanding.   This corresponds with the nature of the work of the Spirit as Founder of relations *par excellence*.   As I indicated before, the Spirit founds the relation between me and the others.   Men, fellow believers of mine participated in the making of the Bible. They experienced God.   They have testified it.   And they have described it.   All that belongs to the one, great event of the acting of the Spirit.   But that acting of the Spirit goes on.   I come in touch with the Bible, *via* the proclamation of the Gospel or *via* other causes, and anew the Spirit comes into play to connect me with God in Christ, *via* the Scripture and *via* the

so gelehrt sein, das Neue Testament nicht ganz verstehen nicht kongenial interpretieren.' Karl Barth also desired a 'Kongenialitat mit den Zeugen der Offenbarung', cf. his *Die Christliche Dogmatik im Entwurf,* Munchen, 1927, p. 408. G. Maier, to whom I am indebted for these references, uses and defends the idea 'congeniality' in a sense which already encloses the knowledge with respect to the understanding of faith.

35. *Cf.* J. Firet on the operation of the Spirit through men in his *Het agogisch moment in het pastoraal optreden*, Kampen, 1974, pp. 154-176.   See also M. Barth, *Conversation with the Bible*, New York-Chicago-San Francisco, 1964, pp. 293-298, about 'The Spirit and Bible Study'.

men who come to the Word in the Scripture. So the Spirit places me in a *Ich-Du* relation, which God will maintain with men. This relation is brought about in the knowledge of God in Christ, which itself is owed to the illumination of the Spirit. For illumination, revelation and knowledge in Biblical thinking are no purely cognitive, intellectual concepts. God's revelation is not only a communication about God and his salvation. Rather God communicates in Scripture *himself* and his salvation. There God in his revelatory activity is not only dealing with the intellect but with the whole man. Just so is the knowledge of God, which is given to man by illumination, not only a taking notice of God and his work, but rather the annexation of his thinking and willing and working.[36] Illumination, revelation, knowledge are therefore 'relational' just because they are existential.

This knowing is a tremendous thing, comparable with creation itself, *cf.* 2 Cor.4:6. Just as creation has the spirit of God as its author so the recreation has as its author the Spirit of God, who is now the Spirit of Christ. The knowledge which a man like Paul had of Christ, has as its fundament of possibility his renewal, caused by the Spirit (Acts 9:17). The Holy Spirit is ready to grasp, transform and fill also the present interpreter, This does not mean the deprivation and elimination of all existing exegetical methods. It means no more, as I indicated before, the necessity of a new, pneumatical method.[37] I will quote with agreement a statement of Thomas F. Torrance, who stresses that our knowledge of God is a *human* knowledge. He says: 'Are we to think of this as somehow heightened or spiritualised until it becomes supra-rational or ecstatic? Surely not, for it is the miraculous nature of the Spirit's activity that while he creates in us the ability to know God beyond all creaturely and human capacities this does not involve any suppression of our rational and critical powers. If we are

---

36. *Cf.* K. Barth, *Kirchliche Dogmatik* IV, 3, Zollikon-Zürich, 1959, p. 586.

37. It can be noted that most pleas for a 'pneumatic exegesis' in fact intend to plead for a 'pneumatic interpreter'.

enabled to apprehend God in his own divine nature, it is without having to take our feet off the ground, so to speak, or without having to transcend our human nature in space and time. In no way are we asked to take leave of our senses or to make irrational steps.'[38]

Also in this connection we must take into account that the Spirit does not supress our humanity, but rather will employ it in his own work. To that humanity belongs also those possibilities and methods which are at our disposal. It is not devalued but honoured. Meanwhile this does not exclude, but rather includes, that the work of the Spirit in, with and through us will influence the way in which we as interpreters use the various methods.[39]

So it is the Spirit who enables us to find the true understanding and so the right interpretation.[40] And because the Spirit is the Author, we have to pray: *Veni creator et recreator Spiritus, veni et illumina nos!* Come and illumine us! It is the same prayer which was uttered by the Psalmist, saying: 'Open thou mine eyes, that I may behold wondrous things out of thy law' (Ps.119:18).

---

38. Torrance, *op.cit.*, p. 275.
39. Therefore is to be welcomed the way in which the New Testament scholar P. Stuhlmacher (Tübingen) in several publications connects 'Spirit' and 'method'. Interesting for this viewpoint is also the contribution of F. Martin, 'The Charismatic Renewal and Biblical Hermeneutics', in John C. Haughey, S.J., ed., *Theological Reflections on the Charismatic Renewal. Proceedings of the Chicago Conference October 1-2, 1976,* Ann Arbor, Mich., USA, 1978, pp. 1-37.
40. M. Barth, *op.cit.*, sees as criterion for the righteousness of someone's exegesis the effects of it on other people.

A CHRISTIAN THEOLOGIAN:
CALVIN'S APPROACH TO THEOLOGY

Revelation in the Old and New Testaments

RONALD S. WALLACE

Though God has given a clear revelation of himself in the created world around us, and we all have an 'instinct' for religion which should lead us towards him, our natural perversity of mind makes it impossible for us to profit from natural religion until we have first of all come to know him through Holy Scripture.

Early in history, therefore, God chose a nation – a people of God who were to be drawn even then into a 'close and intimate relation to himself' (*Inst.* 1:6:1). He came near to representatives chosen from it. He spoke his Word to them, giving them his presence in a special way and revealing himself. As he did so, he changed their inner mind and attitude by his Spirit so that they become reconciled and receptive to the truth. Thus, one nation on earth began to know and to call on the true God. The Old Testament shows how through the centuries God lovingly and patiently brought the light of his Word in marvellous ways to the patriarchs, to Moses and the prophets, in preparation for Christ. The New Testament is the account of the same Word given to the apostles who witnessed to Jesus the Word made flesh (*Inst.* 1:6.1: 8:3-13).

The record of all the events and words which make up this work of God spanning the centuries has been preserved for us in the Old and New Testaments. It pleases God that we ourselves should come to know and experience the truth of God today only through the witness of those inspired prophets, writers and apostles to whom we owe this book. 'It is impossible,' writes Calvin, 'for anyone to enjoy the smallest portion of sound doctrine, unless he is taught by Holy Scripture' (*Inst.* 1:6:2).

When, however, we become responsive to the Word of God and are receptive to Holy Scripture, then we begin to be delivered from the 'depraved judgement' which originally vitiated our approach to nature, and we can now turn back to the natural world with a newly found ability to discern there the witness to God which we had previously excluded from our lives. Aided by Scripture, as eyes dimmed with age and weakness become aided by spectacles, we can begin to recognise what is truly before us in the world around us (*cf.* Introductory Argument to *Commentary on Genesis, CTS* transl., p.62; *Inst.* 1:14:1).

Holy Scripture is given to us in order that through its witness we might not only be given true and reliable statements about God, but also in order that we might also share in the personal knowledge of God which is at the heart of his self-revelation. In a short but significant paragraph in the first chapter of the *Institutes*, entitled in our most recent edition, *'Man Before God's Majesty'*, Calvin quotes a series of biblical texts to remind us of the 'dread and amazement' with which 'holy men were struck and overwhelmed whenever they beheld the presence of God'.

He reminds us of Job, Abraham, Isaiah and Elijah all overcome with a sense of their own folly, feebleness and corruption, as they became conscious that the living God himself had drawn near to them. This is, for Calvin, the kind of situation, or position, in which a true knowledge of God can take place and in which theology becomes possible. What we read of in Holy Scripture as happening to Old Testament men in the field, or in the temple, must now happen to us in our very different circumstances today. We must be able to say not simply that we know the book, its truth and its teaching, but that through its ministry we too have stood in the presence of our maker and redeemer, have heard his voice and have been given the same intimate knowledge of his will and nature as our forefathers in the faith.

It is within the church, as the pastor fulfils his holy ministry in Word and sacrament, that God draws near to us as he did to them. 'God himself appears ... and requires his presence to be recognized in our midst'. Even though such a treasure is given to us in 'earthen vessels', nevertheless in the hearing of the preached Word within the Church we hear the same voice as they heard. We 'listen not only to his ministers speaking but to himself'. So real and personal is his presence in such an encounter today that to deny or resist it would be like blotting out the face of God which indeed shines through such teaching' (*Inst.* 4:1:5 ; *cf. Commentary* on 1 Cor.4:7).

In discussing how God has been able to bring himself, whether under the Old or the New Covenant, into such personal dealing with the individual that he can become known in this close and intimate way, Calvin uses the doctrine of accommodation. If God drew near and showed himself to any of us as he is in his naked glory and greatness, 'his incomparable brightness would bring us to nothing' (*Commentary* on Exodus 33:20). We would be overwhelmed completely in our sinfulness, and would be incapable of grasping anything of his greatness. Therefore in his approach to men in the Old Testament he 'accommodated himself to their capacity' and 'assumed the kind of form they were able to bear', clothing himself in various signs and symbols. In a similar way today, he draws near when the Holy Scripture is preached within the church, and the sacraments are being administered, and uses the audible human speech and visible actions which are offered in the service of his name to veil his presence and communicate his grace – just as he used the symbols and signs of the older dispensation. Thus today God 'appears in our midst', 'allures us to himself', 'displays and unfolds his power to save' (*Inst.* 4:1:5). For Calvin therefore Holy Scripture, as the Word of God to us, is not only an infallible source of true doctrine but also an instrumental means of God's self-revelation. God's Word, spoken in this personal way, creates faith in the minds and hearts of those who hear. Since God in his Word offers friendship and makes promises, personal trust is always an important element in our response to him.   Calvin's definition of faith describes it as 'a firm and sure knowledge of the divine favour towards us founded in the free promise of Christ, revealed to our minds, and sealed in our hearts by the Holy Spirit' (*Inst.* 3:2:7).

The Mystical Element in our Knowledge of God

The mention here of the work of the Holy Spirit in revealing the divine favour to our minds, and sealing the truth in our hearts, leaves room for consideration of what we can justifiably call a 'mystical' element in Calvin's experience and understanding of our knowledge of God.   We can understand this best if we note the attention which he paid to the element of vision on our part when revelation takes place.   Certainly Calvin stressed the auditory element in our experience of the Word of God.   'True acquaintance with God', wrote Calvin, 'is made more by the ears than by the eyes' (*Commentary* on Exodus 33:19).   When God uses visual elements alongside the spoken Word in his earthly approach to men, Calvin notes that these are there usually to 'confirm and ratify the truth of his Word' (*Commentary* on Numbers 12:6).

Calvin struggled in his mind to do justice to the biblical accounts of certain theophanies – experiences in which men are said to have seen 'the heavens opened' and to have been given 'visions of God'.   These phrases are, for example, used by Ezekiel to describe his experience by the river Chebar, but they could also apply to incidents in the careers of Jacob, Moses, Isaiah, in the Old Testament, and of Stephen in the New Testament.   In his *Commentary* on Ezekiel's vision Calvin interprets the phrase 'The heavens were opened' metaphorically ('not that they are opened in reality'), yet he insists that the whole account of the incident must be taken to signify an important experience of seeing.   Ezekiel was indeed given an inner eye to see, behind and beyond normally visible reality.   'Removing every obstacle', God 'allows the eye of the faithful to penetrate even to his celestial glory' (*Commentary* on Ezekiel 1:2).   Calvin compares Ezekiel's experience to that of Stephen whose eyes, at the hour of his martyrdom 'were doubtless illumined with unusual powers of perceiving far more than men can behold (*Ibid*).

Calvin therefore does not regard Ezekiel's experience of vision as being peculiar to his day and calling. It was, rather, 'something continuous which was always to exist in his kingdom'. Joel's prophecy, he reminds us (*Commentary* on John 1:15, and on Joel 2:28), implies that under the New Covenant we ourselves should excel the old in matters of vision. Stephen, for example, was given 'other than earthly eyes so that by their peculiar sight they may fly all the way up to the glory of God' (*Commentary* on Acts 7:55). We ourselves are meant to look beyond the earth and raise our thoughts to God himself (*Inst.* 1:1:2). Like Nathaniel we are all meant to 'see the heavens opened' when we look at the Son of Man (*Commentary* on John 1:51). 'What happened then is perpetually living'.

The experience of the ordinary Christian in the presence of God or the living Christ cannot, then, be adequately described simply as one of hearing. It was also one of 'seeing' or 'tasting' or of being 'lifted up into heaven'. Calvin had exalted views of what happened to Isaiah during his vision in the temple. According to his capacity he was allowed to 'perceive the inconceivable majesty of God'. Yet what happened then to Isaiah happens today to Christians when God reveals himself to them: 'There is no absurdity in supposing that God comes down to men today in such a manner as to cause some kind of mirror to relect his glory' (*Commentary* on Isaiah 6:1). By the earthly means which he often uses in revealing himself to us, God seeks to 'bear us up as if in chariots to his own heavenly glory which with its immensity, fills all things, and in height is above the heavens' (*Inst.* 4:1:5).

In describing the nature of our knowledge of God Calvin therefore quite often speaks of the penetrating and comprehensive power of faith through the Spirit – its ability to

127

soar on to a realm beyond the reach of human understanding, and to contemplate God himself. 'When we are drawn (i.e. by the Spirit) we are both in mind and heart raised up far above our own understanding. For the soul, when illumined by him, receives, as it were, a new eye enabling it to contemplate heavenly mysteries by the splendour of which it was previously dazzled.' And it happens that man's understanding, irradiated by the light of the Holy Spirit, begins to taste those things which pertain to the kingdom of God. Previously it had been too foolish and stupid to relish them (*Inst.* 3:2:34).

Even as we meditate on the nature of the Trinity we are reminded by Calvin that God offers himself to our faith not only to be heard and trusted, but to be contemplated (*Inst.* 1:13:2), and we are urged to 'look upon the one God, to unite with him, and to cleave to him' (*Inst.* 1:13:6). In one important passage Calvin seems to be giving us a carefully worded description of his own experience. 'When we call faith "knowledge" we do not mean the kind of comprehension we have of things which normally fall under human sense perception. It is a knowledge so much superior that the human mind has to go beyond and rise above itself in order to attain it. Even where the mind has attained, it does not comprehend what it feels. But while it is persuaded of what it does not grasp, it understands more by the certainty of its persuasion than it could discern of any human matter by its own capacity' (*Inst.* 3:2:14).

Calvin attributes such experiences not to the exercise or discipline of our natural 'spiritual' faculties such as, *e.g.*, transcendental meditation might involve, but to the grace of God and the work of the Holy Spirit in us, as we come to be in Christ. Such experiences, he affirms, are due to the fact that God himself 'comes down to us in order to be near to us ... to bear us up as in chariots to his heavenly glory'. It is the Holy Spirit who thus lifts us up to see. 'Our mind is too rude to be able to grasp the spiritual wisdom of God revealed to us through faith.... But the Holy Spirit by his illumination, makes us capable of understanding those things which would otherwise far exceed our grasp ' (*Inst.* 4:1:5).

In the incarnate life of Jesus his glory was, though present, 'unknown to most because of their blindness', and was seen 'only by those whose eyes the Holy Spirit had opened', so today even though God may be present with the signs which can admit us to a vision of his glory, we too remain blind until we are beamed by the light of the Holy Spirit' (*Commentary* on John 4:14, *Institutes* 3:2:34).

We have called this aspect of our knowledge of God 'mystical' because we have found a phraseology like that which Calvin uses to describe it often also used by writers like Richard of St Victor, Tauler, Bernard, Gregory Palamas, Thomas Merton, and we feel certain that if students of mysticism could overcome the prejudices which the current traditional picture of Calvin tends to create in our minds, then they might find something akin to themselves. We assume that Calvin, in these accounts, was using such language because from his reading he felt it best fitted his own experiences. Such experiences may date from the moment of his conversion. We note in his short autobiographical account of this event the use of the word 'taste' and the reference to a 'knowledge' which 'inflamed a desire to make progress' (see Introduction to *Commentary* on Psalms).

Our Basic Dependence on the Written Word

Calvin often reminds us that we cannot expect to find the Holy Spirit at work in our midst, if we in any way neglect or despise Scripture which is, after all, the 'school of the Holy Spirit' (*Inst.* 3:21:3). 'The Holy Spirit so inheres in his truth, which he expresses in Scripture, that only when its proper reverence and dignity are given to the Word does the Holy Spirit show forth his power' (*Inst.* 1:9:3). We cannot expect our minds to be raised up heavenwards by the Spirit and to be enlightened with vision unless we make the Word of God and its accompanying sacraments, as it were, the door at which we must wait for this gracious elevation of mind and heart. This requirement is brought out in Calvin's exposition of the story of Jacob at Bethel. Undoubtedly Jacob in this experience 'seeing God' 'penetrated into heaven'. Yet, the kingdom of heaven which Jacob entered in vision is opened to us when the Word of God is preached. The sacraments 'can be called the gate of heaven because they admit us into the presence of God'. Word and sacraments together, 'those helps of faith ... by which God raises us to himself, can be called the gates of heaven' (*Commentary* on Genesis 28:17). The implication is that we cannot enter except by this door.

Besides underlining our dependence on the written Word in relation to the dynamic and mystical elements which enter our knowledge of God, Calvin also continually reminds us of our complete dependence on Holy Scripture for all trustworthy teaching and reliable historical information. Nothing can be added to this teaching. 'Let this be a firm axiom. No other word is to be held as the Word of God, and given a place in the church, than that which is contained first in the law and the prophets, and secondly, in the writings of the apostles: and the only accepted way of teaching in the church is by the prescription and rule of his Word' (*Inst.* 4:8:8). To bypass this word is 'to walk where there is no path, and to seek light in darkness' (*Inst.* 3:2:21). To deviate even a hair's breadth from the direction of their word is 'to cast yourself of your own accord into a labyrinth' (*Commentary* on 1 Peter 1:19; *Commentary* on John 3:33).

Faith Seeks Understanding

Calvin's comment on Moses' immediate reaction to the sign of God's presence at the burning bush helps us to understand why he himself tried, after his conversion, to devote his life to the study of theology. 'And Moses said, "I will turn aside and see this great sight". Let us learn then, by the example of Moses, as often as God invites us to himself by any sign, to give diligent heed, lest the proffered light be quenched by our own apathy' (*Commentary* on Exodus 3:3).   Holy Scripture challenges us as the burning bush did Moses, to continued theological reflection.   It demands our interpretation so that its manifold wisdom can be displayed in all its wealth, beauty, clarity and unity.   'How wonderful it is', writes Calvin, 'when we are given confirmation through more intense study, of how admirably the economy of the divine wisdom contained in it is arranged and disposed; how perfectly free the doctrine is from everything that savours of earth; how beautifully it harmonizes in all its parts, how many other qualities give an air of majesty to its composition' (*Inst.* 1:8:1).   Calvin pursued his task as a theologian in the belief that the unity and rationality of God himself must inevitably be reflected in the Word he has spoken in Holy Scripture.   The theologian seeks to bring out the order and system which are hidden there amidst the profusion of its stories and statements, and the apparent confusion of its truths, and he should find joy in doing so.

The theologian, even when he is absorbed in working with the book, will not be able to forget that Holy Scripture is the means by which God himself seeks to draw near to him in his work, and is the door through which his mind has been lifted up to the same kind of vision which characterised the biblical writers themselves.   'What our mind entraces by faith is in every way infinite' (*Inst.* 3:2:14), wrote Calvin speaking as a theologian. He also speaks in this respect of our receiving the eye to contemplate what cannot be reached by normal ways of thought, and of a knowledge *(scientia)* which is superior to all understanding *(notitia),* unreachable by the acuteness of our intellect (*Commentary* on Ephesians 3:18; *cf.. Inst.* 3:2:14, 34). The theologian in his work must seek to grapple in his mind with what his faith has thus seen.   He must expect clarification of the vision to follow the vision, as Christ demonstrated when he cured the man at Bethsaida from his blindness.

The movement of Calvin's mind in his theological thought is therefore well described by Anselm: 'The Christian ought to advance through faith to knowledge, not to come through knowledge to faith, nor, if he cannot know, recede from faith. But when he is about to attain to knowledge he rejoices; and when unable, he reveres that which he is unable to grasp.[1] His theology can therefore be defined as 'faith seeking understanding'. He would have agreed that the chief task of the theologian is not to discover, but rather to clarify the truth that is already given to us in its fullness in the gospel. Such clarification can help, of course, to assimilate the truth into our minds, and eventually to apply it to our lives and to the activity of the church. It can, however, apart from practical results be justified for its own sake. In the course of clarification deeper vision is attained. As Augustine put it, 'We believe in order to understand'.

Away from Ourselves!

Calvin was always aware that in the pursuit of theology, what most hinders arrival at the truth lies not in any obscurity attaching to the revelation, or even to Holy Scripture, but in the natural limitation and perversity of the mind of the theologian. We all have within us a 'lust to devise new and strange religions'. In trying to understand what is before us we tend to work under the bondage of our own 'depraved judgement' and we lose the truth in the 'labyrinth of our minds' (*Inst.* 1:6:3). Though we may profess the faith, and by the grace of God have made some progress in the Christian way, there nevertheless still lurks within each of us a natural spirit, resistent to truth and self-centered – an autonomous human mind. By the sheer bias of our nature even in face of the open Bible, our 'perverted ardour' (*cf. Inst.* 4:17:25) takes control, and we conjure up for ourselves imaginary pictures of God, make him such as our reason conceives him to be, 'reducing him to the level of our low condition' (*cf. Commentary* on Romans 1:21-2). Fascinated by what we can produce from our own thoughts, we become so busy seeking what does not exist that we can fail to

---

1.   Quoted by R. Seeberg, *History of Dogma,* Grand Rapids, 1977, Vol. II, p. 57.

find what does exist (*Inst.* 3:23:2). Most dangerous of all is our tendency always to drag God down to the evil of our own minds and our logic and to imprison him within our own subjectivity.

Calvin was well aware that under the impact of revelation we enter a new experience of self-awareness. The light which comes to us imparts a new quality even to our subjectivity. When we have seen God, 'we begin to feel and know what we are' (*Commentary* on Isaiah 6:5). Calvin refers to this bi-polar aspect of revelation in the opening words of his*Institutes*: 'Nearly all our wisdom, in so far as it can be regarded as true and solid, consists of two parts: the knowledge of God, and of ourselves' (*Inst.* 1:1:1). So vivid does our self-consciousness become under the impress of revelation that we are tempted to confuse what is being presented to us from the direction of objectivity with what is revealed in our own subjectivity: 'While joined by many bonds, which one precedes and brings forth the other is not easy to discern'. The danger now is that man within this rich disclosure situation will begin to lose sight of what should have priority, give way to his inherent self-centredness and become absorbed in examining himself. He will thus destroy the bi-polarity. He will again confuse the objective truth with his subjective experience of it, and his knowledge of God will become false and unsound. Therefore the first rule to be absorbed by the theologian or interpreter of Holy Scripture must always be that of self-denial. We find Calvin enunciating this rule as he describes his own practice in exegesis: we do not with preposterous fervour rashly and without discrimination seize upon what *first* springs to our minds; but after careful meditation upon it, we embrace the meaning which the Spirit of God suggests. Holding on to it we look down as from a height on whatever opposition may be offered by earthly wisdom. Indeed we hold our minds captive, not allowing even one little word of protest, and humble them that they may not presume to rebel (*Inst.* 4:17:25).

It is of course only by the grace of God that we are enabled to deal forcibly enough with our inner bias to falsehood in this matter. This is why Calvin insists that theology must always be done in the presence of the living God himself who alone can subdue our minds to his truth (*Inst.* 1:1:2). In his *Commentary* on Daniel he discusses the vivid picture of what happened to the prophet when he collapsed before the 'great vision' of the man clothed in linen, and when his appearance became abject and pitiful, and he confessed: 'I did not retain my vigour'. Calvin's comments at this point seem to be specially directed to the problem we are discussing. 'We ought to learn to transfer this instruction to ourselves, not by the vanishing of our vigour, or the changing of our appearance whenever God addresses us, but by all our resistance giving way, and all our pride and loftiness becoming prostrate before God. Finally our carnal disposition ought to be reduced to nothing ... all our senses mortified ... for we must always remember how hostile all our natural thoughts are to the will of God' (*Commentary* on Daniel 10:8).

In the presence of the living Word of God, our minds are not only subdued by the brilliance of the light that comes through to them, they are also opened and lifted up to find a new centre of gravity. Calvin reminds us of how the faith we are given by the Word and Spirit, in the presence of God, can deliver and transport our mind entirely away from ourselves into the Word.

Luther had already often given expression to the liberating power of faith in this connection in unforgettable language: 'And this is the reason why our theology is certain', he wrote, 'it snatches us away from ourselves and places us outside ourselves, so that we do not depend on our own strength, conscience, experience, person, or works but depend on that which is outside of ourselves and places us outside of ourselves, that is, on the promise and truth of God, which cannot deceive'.[2] Calvin echoed the same thing in less

---

2. *Luther's Works*, Vol. 27, p. 387.

dramatic style: he points out that as we deny ourselves the Holy Spirit gives us the power to surpass ourselves. He pictures the mind of man as rising up and going 'beyond itself' as it attains the knowledge given to its faith. We do not posses the things of our salvation, he affirmed, unless we can 'transcend the reach of our own intellect and raise our perception above all worldly objects and, in short, surpass ourselves' (*Inst.* 3:2:14, 3:2:41).

He therefore decisively rejected the theological method which would begin with the analysis of our self-consciousness (or our own inner God-consciousness) and would decide the shape of objective doctrine as the soul reflects on its own experience. Though it is not always easy to disentangle what belongs to our self knowledge from what belongs to God. Calvin insists that by the grace of God, and the power of the Spirit we can correct our inner bias to distort and confuse the different elements in the revelation presented to us, and thus quite clearly to discern 'the right order of teaching' which is of course the right order for our theological study (*Inst.* 1:1:1-3). This is that our whole attention should from the beginning be taken up not with our own impressions or feelings but with the reality with which we are confronted when God reveals himself.

Calvin's theological method in this respect is perfectly expressed in words written some years ago by a Roman Catholic theologian. 'If God is God and infinitely richer in reality than ourselves, and if he communicates a word which is rich with his own life and truth, spelling again for us, it is essential that we on our part should submit to be mastered by it, to be drawn up into it instead of dragging it down into ourselves and interpreting it by our own measure of life and experience. That is to say, the test of a divine message is that it should command us and work its way in us without gloss and contamination, and the most disastrous temptation that we can suffer is to desire to test it by our own experience'.[3]

---

3.   M. C. Darcy, *The Nature of Belief*, London, 1931, p. 246.

Calvin's stress as a theologian is, therefore, always on what is before our minds rather than on what is within our minds as an independent and exalted object of our knowing, and in such a way that there can be no confusion between God himself and our own subjectivity. We would imagine also from other aspects of Calvin's thought and teaching that he would regard revelation as an event in which God linked himself up with what is objective in the sphere of human knowledge and human reality – just as he assumed 'flesh' in the incarnation. In his doctrine of Word and sacraments, for example, Calvin regards the eternal Word of God as presenting himself to be heard and received, not merely subjectively but decisively within objective reality.

Even in the ecstatic experience of contemplation to which we have given the name 'mystical', this uniquely sharp subject-object relationship between God and ourselves in which God is sovereign, is not impaired or destroyed. We have seen that in such experience too, it is by the Holy Spirit that we are raised above the earth, and are enabled to contemplate what exceeds our understandings (*Inst.* 3:2:34). Calvin speaks as if the knowledge given to us in such an experience is a knowledge in which the human mind is passive – a knowledge impressed on it by what is contemplated. He speaks of the mind as being 'beamed by the light of the Holy Spirit', of the Spirit as making entry for the Word of God, of the mind as 'absorbing the Word' and as becoming 'endowed with thought' (*Inst.* 3:2:34, 3:2:36).

It is at this point that we can understand most fully what Calvin meant when he said 'All right knowledge of God is born of obedience' (*Inst.* 1:6:2). He speaks at times of a compulsive pressure on the mind as it feels itself under the impact of revelation. We become 'profoundly affected' as 'we feel within ourselves the force of it' (*Inst.* 1:5:9). He confesses that his mind is not simply 'overwhelmed' but also 'conquered'. This suggests that the mind is taken under control by its object, as it tries to shape its new thoughts. It follows in its thinking the patterns inherent in the revelation before it. 'The pious mind', writes Calvin, 'does not dream up for itself any god it pleases, but contemplates the one and only true God. And it does not attach to him whatever it pleases, but is content to hold him as he manifests himself; furthermore the mind always exercises the utmost diligence and care not to wander astray, or rashly and boldly to go beyond his will' (*Inst.* 1:2:2). As C.C.J. Webb puts it: 'The mind is so completely informed by its object that there is as little as possible in the notion we have of the object which belongs to our way of apprehending it and not really to the object itself'.[4]

The Search for System and Definition

Calvin regarded his task always as that of rendering a faithful and systematic account of the teaching of Holy Scripture. The theologian is and must always remain a man before the Bible. No experience is genuine which lifts his mind beyond its control. Holy Scripture, Calvin affirmed, is 'the school of the Holy Spirit'. It is impossible for anyone to enjoy any true inspiration or even the smallest portion of sound doctrine unless he is taught by it. It must become our only guide and our only light. We must not 'speak our guess or even seek to know ... anything except what has been imparted to us by God's word' (*Inst.* 1:21:3, 1:16:2, 3:21:2, 1:14:4).

It is often asserted that Calvin had a naturally systematizing and logical mind, and that it was by applying his logical power to the mass of data given within the texts of Scripture before him that he produced the theological system known as 'Calvinism'. Students of Calvin have sometimes tried to analyse his *Institutes* in order to find the principles he used in producing such a system. Various central principles such as predestination or the sovereignty of God have been suggested. It has been suggested, for example, that his theological discussion was dominated by his desire to give a balanced account of the

---

4: *Problems in the Relations of God to Man,* London, 1915, p. 45.

various contradictions of opposites which are found among the biblical texts. Certainly Calvin tried to be systematic in his theological presentation of the whole gospel, since he believed in the unity and rationality of the Word of God. As he wrote his commentaries on the Bible, and thus deepened and expanded his knowledge of the Word, he constantly revised his *Institutes,* rearranging the order of the discussion and altering his text. We believe, however, that Calvin resisted any tendency he might have had to master the biblical material before him, and to mould it into shape by his logical skill or by his own creative intelligence. He always strove, rather, to bring his mind under the shaping power of the objective reality before him, and to find the logic inherent in the revelation itself. He sought to allow his mind to be taken up, by faith, into the Word itself, and to become penetrated by it. He sought thus to produce a system which reflected the rationality of the Word of God.[5]

This meant that, as he worked with the biblical writers, he never forgot that the object of his theology was the One to whom they bore witness. He had to concern himself with God's actions in history, with the whole story of salvation, promised and fulfilled in Christ. He had to try to hear the words of the living Lord who comes to speak today through the Scriptures. Therefore, as he dealt with the texts which occupied his mind and sought to compare one with another, to interrelate the themes they discussed, and to give his thinking direction and coherence, he had to penetrate beyond the words of the writers to the reality to which they witnessed, and to bring his mind under the compelling power which had originally inspired them.

5.　On this point see *e.g.* T. F. Torrance, *Belief in Science and the Christian Life*, Edinburgh, 1980, pp. 4, 9; *Theology in Reconstruction*, London, 1965, pp. 95-6. Simone Weil in *Waiting upon God*, p. 72, writes of 'attention', which she defines as an act of 'suspending our thought, leaving it detached, empty, and ready to be penetrated by the object .... All our thought should be empty, waiting, not seeking anything but already to receive in its naked truth the object which should penetrate it'.

CALVIN'S APPROACH TO THEOLOGY

Calvin's method was simply that of following in his theological thinking the rationality that is inherent in revelation, with confidence in the possibility of a true correspondence between his thinking about God and the reality of God encountered in revelation. He certainly did not regard his theological thinking as something that provided or created rationality over against a revelation that was entirely noumenal or non-rational.

Calvin was always aware of the inadequacy of his language and even of his thought as he tried to fulfil his task as a theologian. He knew that he could not do justice to 'so great a mystery' as the gospel presents. He confessed such feelings specially when he tried to grapple with the mystery of the Lord's Supper: 'Although my mind can think beyond what my tongue can utter, yet even my mind is conquered and overwhelmed by the magnitude of the thing' (*Inst.* 4:17:7). He quoted Hilary, confessing that he shrank from submitting to the peril of human speech what ought to have been kept with reserve within the mind (*Inst.* 1:13:5). He realised that there were many features in the order and arrangement of his doctrines which even after his best efforts inevitably appeared to contradict human logic. Yet he felt challenged to try both to understand and describe, and he believed he could be of service to the church by giving himself to such a task. 'I will give a summary of my views', he resolved, 'I have no doubt as to its truth. I am confident that it will not meet disapproval from the pious heart'. He believed that, like Paul, he would be helped by prayer and the teaching of the Holy Spirit (*Inst.* 4:17:7 and *Commentary* on Ephesians 3:18).[6]

We have to be cautious, therefore, in the way we apply the word 'systematic' to the mind and thought of Calvin. For a thinker to discover definite forms and shapes within what has been a seemingly incoherent mass of inspired thoughts and

---

6. Medieval mystics were sometimes suspicious that theological speculation would simply lead to loss of the power to appreciate divine things by contemplation. Others believed that clarification would lead to deeper vision.

utterances, and for him to be able to give these new and genuine
expressions in a convincing order, does not necessarily imply
that his is a logical and systematising mind, forcing its own
principles and currents of reasoning on the data before him to
give them shape imposed from without. It simply means that
he has a mind sensitive to the realities of the world of life and
thought around him. The 'beautiful' order (*cf. Inst.* 1:8:1) in
which Calvin was able to cast his thought was an order which,
with all the artistry and scientific skill of a good theologian, he
found concealed in the revelation which had come to him. He
had delight and joy in faithfully preserving it as he brought it to
light. Calvin certainly brought precise and exact thinking into
the decisions he made and the work he did. But it was thinking
done by a man whose mind had been totally 'subdued' and
'made tractable', (see Calvin's account of his conversion in his
Introduction to *Commentary* on Psalms) under the impact of the
Word of God. It has been argued that those who subjected
Reformed theology to logical thinking and to the basic principles
of their own minds were the later successors of Calvin and of
Luther too, the men especially of the third generation.   In
seeking to fulfil the task Calvin remained always aware that
even in achieving clarity there must be no violation of the
essential mystery that must always remain at the heart of
everything, where God is active, present and personal. But it
was precisely because of such mystery that clarity was all the
more necessary, not in thinking *through* the mystery of the
faith, but in thinking *round* it, in showing where it lies, how
great it is and must remain, and in opposing the false doctrines
that might obscure it. Even the mystery would be weakened
and obscured by irrationality and by careless thinking and
language.   On one occasion Calvin wrote Pierre Viret
instructions to give to the Dean of his area as to the attitude he
should adopt in the discussions that were then taking place over
the sacrament: 'let him fearlessly set aside all unreasonable
views, in replying to them and warning them, taking care that he
does not weaken the truths in so doing. Nor is it allowable to
complicate by ambiguous and obscure language what requires
the utmost clearness or perspicuity' (*Letter* to Viret, August

1542). He himself achieved this aim. Someone said of him, 'There is hardly perhaps a sentence in his works which requires to be read twice in order to be understood'.

Theology and Godliness

In Calvin's thought and practice we find the same intimate connection between theology, piety and godliness which we find in all the early fathers of the church. The surrender and obedience of the mind to God which make true theology possible involve the surrender and obedience of the whole life to God.

'How can it help us, in short, to know a God with whom we have nothing to do? Rather our knowledge should result first to teach us reverence and fear, and secondly, under the guidance of its teaching to ask every good thing from him, and when it is received to ascribe it to him. For how can the idea of God enter your mind without giving rise to the thought that since you are his workmanship you are bound by the very law of creation to submit to his command, and that you owe your life to him?' (*Inst.* 1:2:2). In his description of the Christian life Calvin contrasts the 'philosopher' who assigns to reason the sole direction of conduct, with the Christian philosopher who submits his understanding to the Holy Spirit so that he himself no longer lives, but Christ lives within him. 'We are consecrated and dedicated to God', he reminds us, 'that we may henceforth neither think, nor speak, meditate, and act except to his glory'(*Inst.* 3:7:1).

In seeking our response to his redemptive work God certainly appeals first of all for the response of our intellect to a rationally understood Word. 'The intellect', Calvin taught us, 'is to us the guide and ruler of the soul ... the will always follows its bidding, and waits for its decision in matters of desire' (*Inst.* 1:15:7). Through the mind, however, God seeks also the simultaneous response of will and affections, and there never can be a complete and obedient surrender of the mind to the

Word, unless the other faculties are thus involved. Christianity 'is a doctrine not of the tongue but of the life and is not apprehended merely by the intellect and memory, like other sciences, but is received only when it possesses the whole soul, and finds its seat and habitation in the innermost recesses of the heart' (*Inst.* 3:6:4, *cf.* 3:2:8). We have to pour into the heart what the mind has imbibed, for the Word of God is not received by faith if it merely flutters in the brain' (*Inst.* 3:2:36). From its seat in mind and heart the Word must also 'pass into the conduct, and thus transform us itself so as not to prove unfruitful' (*Inst.* 3:6:4), for when God's truth is encountered it seeks to transform the knower himself. 'We cannot possibly know God if we do not keep his commandments and show ourselves dutiful children and obedient servants' (*Commentary* on 1 John 2:3). Here then is a test for our own theology: 'Truth that does not seek to transform the knower is only the empty ghost of knowledge' (*Ibid*). What was once well said of Augustine could be repeated of Calvin: 'Truth entire entered the whole man'.

The theologian should find himself continually drawn on and inspired in his theological quest by a desire for communion and union with God. He should find himself, as he makes progress, more and more drawn into this quest. 'As soon as the least particle of faith is instilled in our minds we begin to contemplate the face of God, peaceful, serene and showing favour towards us. We see him far off indeed, but still so clearly that we know ourselves to be in no way deluded. Then the more we advance (and we ought assiduously to do so) making steady progress, then our view of things becomes closer and more sure, and as it continues he is made even more familiar to us' (*Inst.* 3:2:19). He thus confesses the ardour he felt in pursuit of this aim: 'Even Plato groping in his darkness felt "ravished" by his idea of the beautiful! How then is it possible to know God and yet be touched with no feelings?' The same Spirit who enlightens our minds when God is known also inspires our hearts with 'an affection corresponding to our knowledge' (*Commentary* on 1 John 2:3). 'To believe with the whole heart', he wrote, 'is not to believe Christ perfectly, but only to embrace him from the heart with a sincere mind, not to be filled with him, but with ardent affection to hunger and thirst and sigh after him' (*Inst*.4:14:8; *cf. Commentary* on Acts 8:3).

The theologian in this search after God finds that his 'mental powers are held in wondering suspense' (*Inst*. 1:5:9). He finds himself so overwhelmed by the greatness and holiness before him that all thought of investigation ceases and he can only adore (*Brève Instruction Chrétienne*, 1537, 1:3). Theology, always near to prayer, passes into it. At one point Calvin quotes Augustine: 'You wish to argue with me? Marvel with me and exclaim, " O depth!" Let us both agree in fear lest we perish in error' (*Institutes* 3:22:10). Blending with this devotional fervour was also the desire for the consummation of those experiences which we have referred to as mystical. These gave Calvin a passion to see and understand more of what he has already been lifted up in heart and mind to contemplate, to taste more of what he has already been given.

All this enables us to place Calvin in his theological quest among those who found themselves, as a recent author put it, 'gripped by an almost biological hunger for fulfilment – for that beatific vision of God, of which faith is the earthly bait'.[7] After all, for Calvin, the whole of the Christian life was to be lived as 'nothing more than a meditation on immortality'. (*Brève Instruction Chrétienne* 1:1). He found his mind as a theologian reflected in a memorable passage which he quotes, again from Augustine: 'We have entered into the way of faith, let us constantly hold to it. It leads to the chambers of the king in which are hidden all the treasures of knowledge and wisdom ... We must walk, we must make progress. We must grow, that our hearts may be capable of those things which we cannot yet grasp. But if the last day shall find us making progress, we shall learn there what is beyond us here' (*Inst*. 3:21:2).

---

7. M. D. Chenu, *Is Theology a Science?*, New York, 1964, p. 30.

Church Theology

It must now be admitted that those aspects of Calvin's approach to theology which we have so far selected for the purpose of our discussion have given such a one-sided description of the man at his work as to be almost deceptive. Calvin, of course, did not approach his task as a solitary scholar of the Bible, with mystical tendencies, concerned to classify his own vision of God, even for the sake of teaching others. For him theology was church theology. The church in his time was threatened by false teaching from within and beset by vicious enemies in the world outside. The theologian was a doctor of the church, called by God into leadership in this critical situation, and charged with the pastoral care of the flock as a whole. The theologian is called by God to leave 'purposeless, speculative study' in order to 'labour in the word and teaching' (*cf. Commentary* on 1 Timothy 5:17). Because such a work was onerous and troublesome he himself had at first shrunk from it till Farel had importuned him to become such a teacher within the church at Geneva. He had wanted rather, at first, to devote himself to a purely academic life. He saw too many theologians in his day who tended to keep themselves apart from the everyday struggles of the church, and he was suspicious that some in his day engaged in theological teaching and discussion simply because they loved to talk and be heard. It is easy for a man within the shady precincts of the school to be a ready talker. 'Many wish to be teachers', he wrote, 'and there is hardly one, who is not anxious to be listened to' (*Inst.* 3:12:1; *Commentary* on Leviticus 1:6; *cf.* James 3:1).

He saw it as most important for the health of the church that there should be teachers within it who can note what is being said in the pulpits, both to criticise errors which might arise in the church, and to listen to new truth from the Word which might help to reform the accepted faith at different points. There is a need here for love, unity and willingness to reform. Calvin can speak of 'an unerring standard both for our speaking and thinking about God' which 'must be derived from Scripture' (*Inst.* 1:6:3). He also sought 'by simple and accurate explanation to render Christian doctrine more and more plain and clear to men, and rid their minds of vague causes of discord' (*cf. Inst.* 4:17:25).

Calvin would, of course, not have thought it possible to fulfil his task as a theologian apart from dialogue and communion with others alongside of him in the fellowship of the church. He attended conferences when he could, entered fellowship with other theologians in the world church, corresponded with them voluminously, gave advice and listened to it. 'God', he once wrote, 'could indeed himself have covered the earth with a multitude of men; but it was his will that we should proceed from one mountain, in order that our desire for mutual accord might be greater, and that each might the more freely embrace the other as his own flesh.' He 'has never so blessed his servants that each possessed pure and perfect knowledge on every part of their subject' (*Commentary* on Genesis 1:28; Dedicatory letter to *Commentary* on Romans). Likewise Calvin knew that to help him to come to the fullest possible insight into the teaching of the Holy Scripture he must put himself into debt to the fathers of the church. A superficial perusal of the *Institutes* will reveal how great that debt was.

Theology in Conflict

We could call Calvin's theology a 'confessional' theology. Truth was a trust committed to him by God to be protected in every way and even at the cost of human life. We must not lessen it in anything. To hide it in any way from others or to present it in less than its fulness, thus diminishing its truth, would be to behave like a thief playing fast and loose with another's property (*Letter to Louis du Tillet*, 31 Jan. 1538). He could not therefore for a moment bear to see or hear it denied or distorted by anyone without going to its defence. 'When I see the heavenly doctrine of Christ, of which he has please to make me a minister, everywhere contemptuously outraged, how disgraceful it would be for me to hold my peace' (*Letter* to the Pastors of Berne, May 1555). The moral and political struggles of the times demanded confession of faith, and for a man to confess his faith required theological thinking and statement. 'How, indeed, can this faith, which lies buried in the heart within, do otherwise than break forth in ... confession?' he wrote to Luther, who himself had written, 'A man becomes a theologian by living, dying and by being damned' (*Letter* to Luther, 21 Jan. 1545).

Calvin therefore felt that the theologians of his age whose views deserved to be listened to with greatest respect were those who had proved the truth of their theology by martyrdom. In Crespin's *History of the Martyrs* there is a remarkable passage in a letter from him to some believers suffering for their faith who had written to him asking for his judgement on their creed – whether its theology was correct or required modification. Calvin's reply shows clearly how little he cared about correctness in an utterance of faith, so long as it was an expression of the boldness and devotion of heart inspired by the Spirit. 'I do not send you such a confession of faith as our good brother required of me, for God will render that which he enables you to frame, according to the will of the Spirit imparted to you, far more profitable than any which might be suggested to you by others. Even when desired by some of our brethren, who shed their blood for the glory of God, to revise and correct the confession which they had made, I was very glad to see it that I might receive edification therefrom: but I would not add or diminish a single word, thinking that any alteration would have diminished the authority and efficacy, which ought to be attributed to the wisdom and constancy which plainly proceed from the Spirit of God'.[8]

For Calvin the first virtue required for a man who would be a true theologian was not learning or cleverness but courage, and time and again he confesses his thankfulness that the grace of

---

8.   Quoted by P. Henry, *Life of Calvin*, Vol. I, p. 295.

God has enabled him to be faithful to the truth and to choose it in the face of danger, in spite of his natural timidity. He once in a letter reproached Melanchthon for his slowness to declare his mind and take a side on an important theological issue. 'While, however, you dread, as you would some hidden rock, to meddle with this question from the fear of giving offence, you are leaving in perplexity and suspense very many persons who require from you somewhat of a more certain sound, on which they can repose; and besides, as I remember I have sometimes said to you, it is not over-creditable to us, that we refuse to sign, even with ink, that very doctrine which many saints have not hesitated to leave witnessed with their blood' (*Letter* to Melanchthon, 28th June 1545).

The same desire to confess and defend the truth lay behind all Calvin's polemical writing. A recent able student of Calvin has expressed some regret that whereas the Reformer 'reserved his elegance of style ... for orthodox theology, he showed his contempt for all deviating teaching with the language of the farmyard or the circus'.[9] Undoubtedly in his polemical writing he at times shocks our modern sensitivity in such matters. When he attacked the Lutheran, Joachim Westphal, in 1556 for his views on the Lord's Supper he used such a spate of vituperative and sometimes bitter language even his hardened opponent complained that he must have tried hard not to omit any kind of insult. Six hundred times, Westphal affirmed, Calvin had called him 'Thou fool!', thus ignoring Christ's dire warnings (Calvin's *Tracts,* vol.2, pp.347, 349).

The use of such a style can be partly explained as simply a fashion of the times. Yet Calvin affirmed that it cost him to assume such a harsh role and that in doing so he was simply deliberately playing his part in the struggle which theological existence involved in his day. He affirmed that he took no pleasure in being 'dragged into the contest'. He wrote later that

---

9.　Peter Cook, 'Understanding Calvin', in *Scottish Bulletin of Evangelical Theology,* Vol. 2, p. 58.

'the harshness of my language has been wrung from me against my will'. In describing how it happened he admits that his zeal had carried him beyond the limits of moderation: 'The book was hastily written. What the case required, and occurred spontaneously at the time, I dictated without any lengthened meditation and with a feeling ... remote from gall .... I had no bitterness in my heart'. Yet he had to make his opponent feel that 'the defenders of truth were not without sharp weapons' (*Letter* to Zerkinden, 4th July 1558; *Tracts*, vol.2, pp.347, 349).

His final line of defence was that Westphal had entered the public arena in order to challenge the truth. In such an arena, hitting and blood-letting were inevitable. If lions and bears have no right to complain of the public reaction to their savage attacks why should this 'delicate little man' himself expect to be treated like a brother when he dared to start playing the game of tearing up the truth of God in public? 'The whole question turns upon this', wrote Calvin, justifying himself – 'Did I attempt to avenge a private injury, or was it in defence of public cause that I strenuously oppose Westphal?' (*Tracts*, vol.2, p.351).

Westphal's writings which were being circulated had, he felt, degraded the ascension glory of Jesus Christ, and given public insult to the Lord. The honour of God was at stake. The church was being threatened. Such attacks demanded a response and the opposition had to be crushed, even ruthlessly. He believed he was justified in treating the enemy 'as if they were savage wild beasts' (*Letter* to Melanchthon, 3rd August 1557).

The Pastoral Aim

Alongside his concern to maintain the truth by public confession, Calvin's pastoral concern never fails to manifest itself in his theological writing. He was led to write the first edition of the *Institutes* with the avowed aim not only to defend the faith against the calumnies of those who were persecuting its followers in France, but also to meet the needs of multitudes who were 'hungering and thirsting after Christ'.

Time and again we find as we read the book the theological argument is interrupted by a short sermon to the reader relating the matter on hand to our daily need, appealing to us to take comfort, and pressing us to make decisions. Equally often he will ask us to join him in an outburst of thanksgiving for the truth he has stated: 'Let us now eagerly triumph in the midst of our troubles .... Let us exult', he cries as he lectures about the final resurrection. Indeed he often composes little hymns woven mostly out of biblical texts but sometimes studded with citations from the fathers – all to help the reader not simply to understand doctrine, but to rejoice in the goodness of God and the all-sufficiency of Christ for every need. When he speaks to us about bearing our cross he pleads with us not to be bitter under our affliction, for he wants us to share the 'cheerful and happy heart' with which he himself is writing these words, and he adds that if we have this joy, we will find ourselves being thankful, even under our cross, and our very thankfulness will produce even more joy.[10]

In the course of the volume we often find the pastoral aim dictating the scope of the discussion. He restrains his mind when it wants to launch out on purely academic speculation. If he can give 'devout leaders' ... enough material to build up their faith it satisfies him (*Inst.* 3:25:3). In his Geneva Catechism he poses the question why the creed only mentions belief in life everlasting and does not speak about hell, and gives the answer: 'Since nothing is held by faith except what contributes to the consolation of the souls of the pious'. In his discussion of predestination, though, he admits that he has to pause over

---

10. *Cf. e.g. Inst.* 3:25:4; 1:17:10-11; 3:8:11. Is it not a valid supposition that the perfect clarity he achieved in his style and exposition was the result of such sheer hard labour to make sure that no reader could be left in uncertainty?

these matters which are being argued by the learned. He wants also to discuss those points which raise 'difficulty for the simple (*Inst.* 3:21:7). At the beginning of the whole discussion we are warned that we are moving into darkness, indeed, into a labyrinth in which souls can become lost, but in which there is 'very sweet fruit' to be found. In the middle of the discussion we are given the advice to make sure that our life has begun with God's call, so that we can end with the same, to turn our eyes to Christ in whom we see 'God's fatherly mercy and kindly heart', and we are urged to let the practice of this doctrine ... also ... flourish in our prayers (*Inst.* 3:24:4-5).

INDEX

152